Barbarossa: invasion of Russia 1941

D1612712

Barbarossa: invasion of Russia 1941

John Keegan

Editor-in-Chief: Barrie Pitt
Editor: David Mason
Art Director: Sarah Kingham
Picture Editor: Robert Hunt
Designer: David Allen
Cover: Denis Piper
Special Drawings: John Batchelor
Photographic Research: Benedict Shephard
Cartographer: Richard Natkiel

First published in the United States of America.
This edition first published in Great Britain
in 1971 by Macdonald & Co, (Publishers) Ltd
49 Poland Street, London W1.

Printed in Great Britain by
Hazell Watson & Viney Ltd, Aylesbury, Bucks

Contents

Clash of arms

Introduction by Barrie Pitt

It is probable that history will regard 22nd June 1941 as the apocalyptic date of the military calendar. No military plan of the scope of Operation Barbarossa had ever before been launched, for never before had techniques of organisation, transport, and communication been available for application on such a scale.

'When Operation Barbarossa is launched,' Hitler proclaimed, 'the world will hold its breath!'

It did not, in fact, for the world is not much interested in matters much removed from personal and almost domestic circles. The opening moves of Barbarossa presented the greatest military spectacle since the events of August 1914, and Western Europe and America watched them with the casual disinterest of cattle watching the passing of an express train. Even those whose profession was the analysis of great affairs were mostly concerned with estimating the degree of attrition to which German strength would be subject before the inevitable collapse of Russian resistance, and as the armoured spearheads cut deep into Russia, it did not seem that Hitler's boast of conquest before Christmas was idle in any way.

'We have only to kick in the front door,' he had told his generals, 'and the whole rotten edifice will come tumbling down!' – and as day followed day and the black lines extended ever farther eastward, the only exaggeration the statement appeared to possess was with regard to the effort needed against the 'front door'. Moreover, the doubt which had always arisen in military minds when they had watched such swift advances in the past did. not now arise. Here, it seemed, was no spectacle of skilful tactical retreats tempting the aggressor ever deeper into a trap – for whole Russian armies were being caught and annihilated. The prison-cages were full to overflowing and within the wide sweeps of the armoured columns, the soil was soaked in Russian blood. Seventeen days after the first onslaught, 300,000 Russian prisoners, 2,500 Russian tanks, 1,400 Russian guns, and 250 aircraft had been captured on Army Group Centre's front alone, while reconnaissance reported quite correctly that many hundreds of Russian aircraft had been destroyed on the ground.

When Army Group Centre was seen to pause on the Desna, therefore, the west took little hope from the spec-

tacle, for it was not unreasonable to believe that Russia's armed might was now smashed or at least trapped and that the Germans were engaged in mopping-up, reinforcing tired but triumphant troops, and preparing for the last easy sweep ahead into Moscow.

To the German troops it did not look quite like that, but at the same time there was little about the position to cause them worry. True, Ivan was building up strength immediately in front, and had already proved to be a stubborn fighter; there was undoubtedly a hard fight still ahead – but victory was the more satisfactory for being hard-won and anyway was quite certain. A fortnight and the advance would begin again, with rested troops, replenished magazines, and replaced vehicles – for these had taken severe punishment over the rough and often almost non-existent Russian roads.

But success brings problems just as surely as failure, and as John Keegan points out in his brilliant analysis of the dilemma which now faced Hitler – at the higher command level, the touch was less sure. Hitler had already said that the most difficult decision of the war could be whether to turn north or south after breaking through the Stalin Line.

To the astonishment of the men on the Desna, therefore, they were now robbed of their pride and their shield, Guderian's Panzer Group, which to their leader's ill-concealed fury was ordered south-west, back towards Kiev, while I Panzer Group was ordered north. And yet another vast series of encirclements began, this time with even greater yields in Russian prisoners and booty, and a victory which in terms of numbers of casualties, constituted the greatest catastrophe in Russian history – and thus the greatest single achievement of German arms – was won.

But something had been lost.

Time.

The Red Army

Whatever Hitler's other motives for his attack on Russia in June 1941, one predominated: his belief in the ease of the task he was undertaking. 'You have only to kick in the door,' he was to tell Runstedt, 'and the whole rotten structure will come crashing down.'

What can have led him to form so erroneous an estimate of his opponent, already the greatest land power in the world, as he well knew from the tally kept by his intelligence service of the number of its soldiers and the quantity of weapons in their hands? In his speeches and writings he had, of course, always argued the natural and unalterable inferiority of Slav to Teuton, but those thoughts were intended exclusively for public consumption. He would never have allowed them to cloud his judgement in matters of real moment. Can he have been influenced by his memories of the Russian Army's performance during the First World War, the most formative period of Hitler's life, when all Germany's greatest victories had been won on the eastern front, the greatest of which, largely unremembered in the West, had brought about Russia's defeat and the surrender of her richest provinces? Perhaps; yet, lamentable though Tsarist generalship had proved at the beginning of that war and wholly defeatist the spirit of their Provisional Government's armies at

were bound to tell.

But Hitler did not intend that there should be a long run. He was convinced that the war could be kept short; in part by the speed and penetrative power with which his panzer forces would operate, in part by the advantages which his generals would win from the mistakes made by the Russians in handling their formations. However much bravery the Russian soldier displayed, he believed, it would be negated by errors of judgement and failures of will at a higher level, errors to which the recent performance of the Red Army in Finland had shown its high command all too prone, and which, he believed, the nature of the command structure made unavoidable.

Russian ineptitude was, of course, legendary. Count von Schlieffen, who had drawn up Germany's plans for war before 1914, had based his calculations upon the Russian general staff's reputation for inefficiency, calculations which in his case had led him to plan launching a knock-out blow against the French while the Russians, their allies, might still be expected to be fumbling their way through the preliminary stages of mobilisation.

It was not, however, upon old-fashioned bumbledom that Hitler counted to expedite his plans (though to have discounted it altogether would certainly have been premature). Rather it was upon a fatal compromise he suspected in the system of military command – a compromise of the command principle itself – which the Bolshevik leaders had introduced, and which Stalin, through the medium of the Army Purge of 1937-38, had recently re-emphasised in a particularly dramatic and destructive form.

In this Hitler was undoubtedly on to something. The question 'Who is to be master?' hangs unspoken between army and government in even the longest established states; in those of recent origin, it tends to provoke

its end, the Russians had, on occasions risen to the heights of military achievement; and just as often in attack as in defence, where traditionally the Russian soldier had shown himself at his best. Hitler, moreover, was historian enough to know that Russia had won the respect of every European power that she had fought, and realist enough to accept that Russia's military strengths-'numbers, space, scorched earth, January and February', to which one should also add the bravery and capacity for self-sacrifice of her soldiers – were inherent in the country and the people, whatever regime stood over them. In the long run these strengths

dispute: where that origin was revolutionary, the dispute often turns violent. If it had not done so in Soviet Russia, a revolutionary state saved from extinction by counter-revolution and foreign invasion only through the exertions of the infant Red Army in the Civil War, it was because the Bolshevik leaders had for the first moments of its existence taken the precaution of providing each Red Army officer (though 'officer' was not the word used, since it had been banned) with a commissar or political deputy to oversee his actions.

A dual system of this type, in which the commissar took precedence over the soldier in areas of political decision and was theoretically his equal for purposes of military decision, was perhaps necessary in the earliest days. To officer the Red Army, which had grown from a handful of trustworthy revolutionary guards to a host of several millions in a very short space of time, the Bolshevik leadership had had for the most part to avail itself of the services of former Tsarist officers, of exactly the same background and training as those in command of the White Armies with

which they were at war. This dependance on Tsarist officers was to continue until well into the 1920s; and even after sufficient numbers of dedicated young communists had joined the army from the new academies, ex-Tsarists were still needed in the upper ranks. By then many had established, apparently to the general satisfaction of the leadership, their loyalty to the revolution and to the Communist state. Notable among them was Tukhachevsky, a former Guards officer, who had risen to command one of the Bolshevik armies in the Civil War at the age of twenty-five. When, after the civil war, many former Tsarist officers no longer needed or wanted by the Bolsheviks were being discharged, Tukhachevsky, who led the advance on Warsaw in 1920 and put down the naval rising at Kronstadt in 1921, was already set on the upward path which would carry him to command of the Red Army in the next decade.

Despite the evidently genuine conversion of officers like Tukhachevsky to the new ideology, and despite the hostility of some root-and-branch Red commanders to the commissar

system, it was this system which the Party insisted on maintaining throughout the 1920s and in the early 1930s. While insisting on its necessity, however, the Party did little to choose suitable candidates for the commissar service or to provide for the education of those already enlisted. As a result the commissar too often remained much the same sort of earnest but dim functionary for whom the more dashing Red leaders of the civil war had found so little patience.

The Soviet officer, on the other hand, under the inspiration of Tukhachevsky and his circle, was steadily out-stripping the commissar in professional skills during this period. Secret co-operation with the German army, which the Germans welcomed because of the privacy provided by Russian training areas for their experiments with equipment forbidden under the Versailles treaty, and which the Russians welcomed for the insight it gave them into new military techniques, had helped to make the Red Army by the early 1930s one of the most progressive in the world: it had begun to experiment with the air-landing of major units, both by aero-

plane and parachute, and with the use of massed formations of tanks, the latter chiefly designs developed from the famous Christie prototypes which Russia bought from their American designer in 1931.

This professionalisation of the Red Army received the apparent seal of party approval in March 1934, when the principle of dual control was at last abolished and the commissar's responsibilities were declared confined to those of political advice and education. In the following year formal titles of rank (abolished during the revolution and replaced by euphemisms like 'command specialists') were re-introduced, including the novel distinction of Marshal, to which the five most important Soviet military leaders were promoted. These were Tukhachevsky; Voroshilov, the Commissar of Defence, old-time political agitator, former member of the First Red Cavalry Army and close associate of Stalin; Yegorov, Chief of Staff and former member of the First Cavalry Army; Budenny, ex-Tsarist NCO turned cavalry general (also formerly of the First Cavalry Army); Blucher, another Tsarist ex-sergeant, a hero of the civil war, sometime military advisor to Chiang-Kai-Shek and commander of the semi-autonomous Army of Siberia.

The increasing professionalism of the officer corps was accompanied within the army itself by a marked shift towards an all-Regular, or more accurately, all-active army. Hitherto the majority of the Red Army's infantry had belonged to Citizen Militia formations based on an urban area, whose soldiers trained only intermittently. This was now changed, the bulk of the infantry divisions being transformed into active formations into which the conscript soldier was inducted to serve his full term of service in one go. To compensate for any consequent scaling-down of facili-

RED ARMY IN 1937, BEFORE THE PURGE

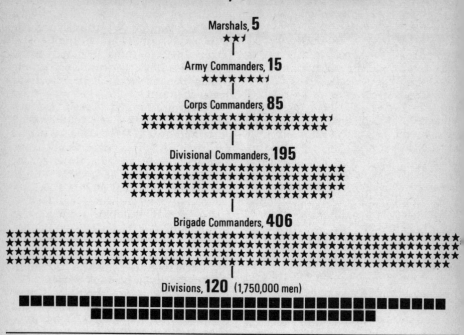

Marshals, **5**

Army Commanders, **15**

Corps Commanders, **85**

Divisional Commanders, **195**

Brigade Commanders, **406**

Divisions, **120** (1,750,000 men)

RED ARMY AFTER THE PURGE

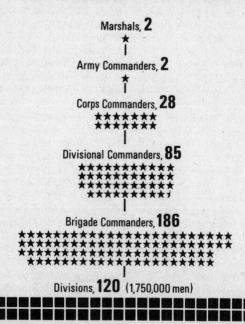

Marshals, **2**

Army Commanders, **2**

Corps Commanders, **28**

Divisional Commanders, **85**

Brigade Commanders, **186**

Divisions, **120** (1,750,000 men)

One symbol represents 2 officers or 2 divisions

ties for the military training of the workers, peasants and town dwellers, larger funds were allocated to the *Osoaviakhim* (Society for the Promotion of Aviation and Chemical Defence). At the same time its leaders were told in a decree signed by Stalin that they must spare no efforts to school the great mass of Soviet citizens in marksmanship, parachute jumping (carried out not from aeroplanes but from special harnesses attached to tall towers), and civil defence.

This increase in the size of the full-time contingent of the Red Army was very much in line with ideas which Tukhachevsky and like-minded Soviet generals had had from the beginning. Its effect was however less efficacious in practice than in theory, for it introduced in larger numbers into the army that class of embittered young peasants who had proved so difficult to train and assimilate since the collectivisation of agriculture began in 1931. So alarmed were some senior officers of the army becoming at the temper of the conscript units that requests were heard from them for some modification of the programme. Marshal Blucher, in Siberia, was actually able to extract concessions. But there was a failure to extend these concessions to the rest of the country.

How, indeed, could Stalin have agreed? Any show of weakness at this stage of his dictatorship might have finished him, so violent and widespread were the hundreds that he accumulated against himself. He had just completed the main part of his great purge of the party and a subsidiary purge of the NKVD (the Secret Police). These two of the three great organs of power within the State were now unquestionably his; the third, the army, still retained the power to topple him should its leaders so choose, and its leaders in the main owed him nothing. Voroshilov, who had held the post of Commissar for War since 1925, appeared loyal, but was also the least professionally military of the five marshals and probably commanded correspondingly less support than any of them among the regular officer corps. The rest, and the bulk of the upper ranks of the Red Army besides, owed Stalin nothing personally. Their careers had already begun before Stalin acceded to power and their promotion had depended more upon their own exertions or the esteem won from their fellows than upon the intervention of the party or the distribution of personal favours. Little wonder that Stalin, now thoroughly excited by the atmosphere generated by the purge within the party, half-believing the dangers he had himself fabricated and perhaps intoxicated by the pleasure of bloodletting for its own sake, should have determined not to stop until all his enemies, real, potential or imagined, had received the bullet in the neck.

It may also be that some firmer evidence of conspiracy against his personal rule was available to Stalin, there existing rumours that the Gestapo had insinuated a fabricated dossier suggesting that Tukhachevsky was exchanging intelligence with the German General Staff. These rumours remain unsubstantiated: nevertheless, Tukhachevsky *had* been behaving unwisely during the party purges, notably during a trip he made to France – an unparalleled indulgence for a Soviet Officer – and more ominously he had also been accused by a defendant during one of the Party show trials of being in touch with Trotsky. Whatever the truth in that, or in any allegations made against him or any other officer, Tukhachevsky was among the first to suffer arrest and death. He and seven generals were tried and shot on June 11-12th, 1937.

This brutal little episode both instituted and characterised the holocaust that was to follow. By the autumn of 1938, as a result both of summary executions and of elaborate show trials, the Red Army had lost between a quarter and a half of its

Stalin

Tukhachevsky

Zhukov

Voroshilov

Budenny

Blucher

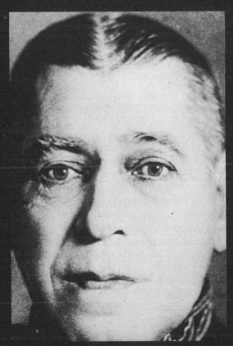

Shaposhnikov

Timoshenko

Russian paratroopers – among the first in the world – undergo equipment training

officers: three out of its five Marshals; thirteen out of fifteen army commanders; fifty-seven out of eighty-five corps commanders; 110 out of 195 divisional commanders and 186 out of 406 brigade commanders. Lower down, it is estimated that the blows fell even thicker, though in the ranks from Colonel to Captain imprisonment was often apparently substituted for execution. But in the most senior command and politico-military appointments, death seems to have been an almost mandatory sentence: all eleven Deputy Commissars for Defence were shot, seventy-five of the eighty members of the Military Soviet, set up in 1934, all Military District Commanders and most of their Chiefs of Political Administration (i.e. senior commissars).

It was difficult, however, to detect any method in Stalin's madness. The purge had certainly got rid of the bloc of ex-Tsarist officers; yet it had also done away with many of the revolutionary commanders who had emerged from the ranks or from nowhere during the Civil War, and at the same time it had left some of the most notable ex-Tsarist officers in their places. Shaposhnikov, who had done his training in the Imperial General Staff College and had been disgraced by Stalin in 1931 was actually appointed by him to succeed Yegorov, whose peasant origins were impeccable, as Chief of Staff in 1937, and succeeded in retaining that post until ill health deprived him of it several years later. Nor was it the case that military commanders suffered more heavily than political, since commissars were executed in equal if not greater numbers. The best cachet for survival seems to have been membership of or association with the 1st Cavalry Army of Civil War times, the anti-Cossack force which had enjoyed Stalin's political support and whose operational methods had aroused the hostility of Tukhachevsky.

It was this 1st Cavalry Army Group which in the aftermath of the purge succeeded to power: Budenny, Timoshenko, Kulik and Zhukov. All enjoyed Stalin's patronage, had previously owed him much and now owed him everything, including their lives. Whether his side of the bargain was as good was more doubtful. In Timoshenko he had a capable if not inspired commander; in Zhukov he had a general whose talents approached genius, but who was as yet too junior for his talents to be allowed to flower. In Budenny he had a highly decorative and soldierly figure but one whose tactical ideas (strategic ideas he certainly did not possess) had never been very profound and were now quite out of date.

In Kulik he had a Head of Ordnance, (successor to Tukhachevsky) whose thinking on equipment problems was almost wholly perverse, extending as it did to the withdrawal of light automatic weapons from the army on the grounds that they were unsuitable for soldiers and to the halting of pro-

duction of anti-tank and anti-aircraft guns. He also misinterpreted the evidence culled by Red Army observers during the Spanish Civil War (in which so much Russian equipment was first given operational trials) on the use of armour, deciding on the basis of his conclusions to disband the large armoured formations that Tukhachevsky had been building and to redistribute the tanks among the infantry in small units. The effect of these miscalculations and, more generally, of the upheavals in which they had their root were not to be perceived outside Russia until 1940, after Stalin had unwisely declared war on Finland.

The genesis of that highly embarrassing debacle lay in Stalin's desire to secure the transfer or lease of Finnish territory lying on the approaches to his Baltic naval bases. Finland's refusal to accede led to a breach of diplomatic relations and, on 30th November 1939, to a full-scale Russian attack up the Karelian Isthmus, the land corridor connecting southern Finland to the Leningrad region. Although launched with considerable superiority of numbers, it was repulsed, as were the attacks across the long Russo-Finnish land frontier above and below the Arctic Circle. It was not until the beginning of February 1940, after the concentration of nearly a million reinforcements, and the prolonged bombardment of the Finns' defended positions in the Mannerheim Line, that the Red Army at last broke through, forcing the Finns to sue for peace a month later. This eventual recovery of much lost face was due to the leadership and command skills of Timoshenko, much superior to those of the original commander on the Finnish front, Marshal Voroshilov, who thereafter returned to work of a political nature for which he was better suited.

The pattern and outcome of the Finnish war, in which for the whole of one winter a nation of three-and-a-

Above: One of Russia's unsuccessful pre-war monster tanks, the T-35. *Left:* The BT-7 an early development of the American prototype. *Below:* T-34 — the Russian wonder tank

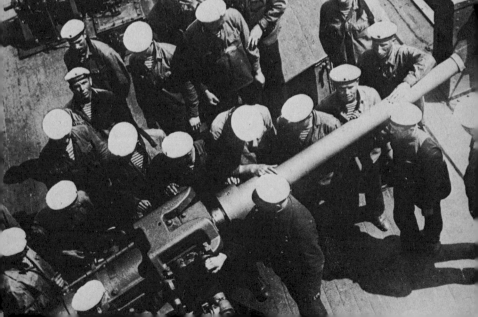

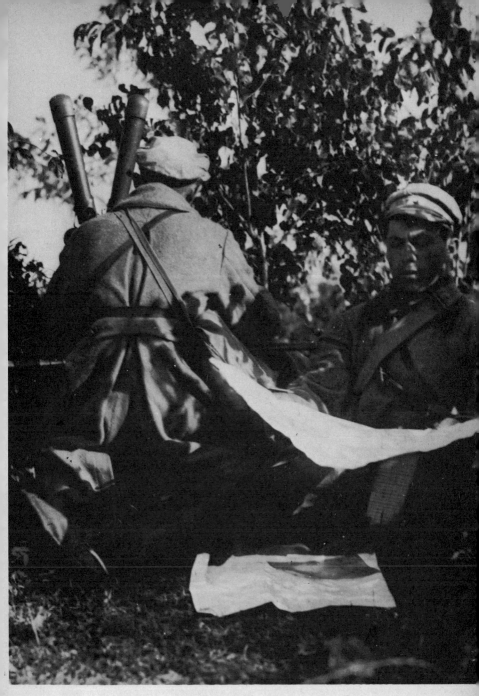

Above left: Russian ski troops on manoeuvres. *Centre left:* Russian 7.62mm light machine gun and crew. *Below left:* Sailors of the Russian Baltic Fleet at gun drill *Above:* Russian artillery observation post – the 'donkey's ears' binoculars were a legacy from the Tsarist army.

Above: A Finnish ski-patrol advances to contact with the Russians, 1939
Below: Finnish soldiers evacuate a position

half million had not merely held back, but run rings round the army of a nation of over one-hundred million, making its leaders look fools in the process, had done little to enhance Soviet military prestige. Indeed so fierce was the enthusiasm aroused in the West by Finland's defiance of the Russians that Britain and France had nearly intervened on her side. Had they done so, they would undoubtedly have regretted the ultimate consequences but the immediate result could only have been further to heighten the Russians' sense of frustration.

In the longer term however, the lessons of the Finnish campaign, if bitter to swallow at once, proved the best medicine that the Russians could have taken. Foreign observers – the most important of whom was Hitler – concluded from the Russians' incompetent performance that their faults – exactly the same faults as they had displayed against an inferior German army in the opening days of the First World War – were incurable; and that in any larger campaign the Russians would suffer the same fate as they had done after the defeats of Tannenberg and the Masurian Lakes twenty-five years earlier. Indolence, ineptitude, lack of foresight, muddle: these were the defects, retrieved only by the bravery of the ordinary soldier, on which any enemy of Russia's might seem safe in counting.

However, Russia – and the Russian Army – had slowly learned how to change. The months that followed the armistice with Finland were months of intensive effort at change. Another campaign, that waged by Zhukov against the intrusive Japanese on the Mongolian border with Siberia, a campaign almost unremarked in the West, had in May 1939 provided evidence quite contrary to that from Finland of what the Red Army was worth. Timoshenko, who now acceded to *de facto* command in place of Voroshilov, set about ensuring that what had been done by a

small detachment of the Red Army in a localised conflict would become the operational standard of the Army as a whole. Zhukov's victory had involved the use of armour in quantity. Timoshenko therefore revived the armoured corps – formations of two tank and one motorised divisions – which Tukhachevsky had organised before his fall. Under his aegis it also proved possible to demote the Commissars, for the second time, to the status of political advisors and to assert the operational independence of the military commander in decision-making. At the same time many of the officers imprisoned or banished during the great military purge were reinstated, and new training and operational regulations, based on the experience of the Russians in Finland and reports of the German conduct of operations in Poland and France, were written and issued.

All that was wrong could not be put right in the available time, short as it was to prove. The purge had dealt a nearly mortal blow to the self-confidence of the officer corps, collectively and individually, making it unlikely that average or below-average officers – by definition the majority – would risk an independent line of action when in contact with the enemy (over-rigid adherence to orders was indeed to prove one of the principal Russian shortcomings). Party propaganda, on the other hand, despite the humiliations of the Finnish War, had an unfortunately inflationary effect on the self-confidence of the ordinary soldiers and in Russian civilian morale, leading its target audience to believe in the invincibility of the Red Army, a belief which was as important an article of political faith as trust in the infallability of the Politbureau's judgement. Nevertheless a very great deal had been achieved by the early summer of 1941 to restore the Red Army to equilibrium, and however much remained to be done, its sheer size and the wealth of its equipment was sufficient to give any potential

Russian activity near the Khalkhin-Gol river. *Above:* Infantry take up stylised poses on a defensive position. *Left:* Russian tanks prepare to advance

attacker pause.

Quite apart from the *Osoaviakhim* and the trained reserves, the latter the product of the system of universal conscription instituted in the mid-1930s, the Red Army in the spring of 1941 had in its order of battle between 230 and 240 divisions, of which most were up to establishment and some 170 were within operating range of the Western frontier. The majority of these were rifle (infantry) divisions of about 14,000 men, which contained little transport and were unmechanised. The tank divisions, of which there were at least twenty-two and perhaps as many as sixty, each consisted of two tank regiments, a lorried infantry and an artillery regiment. Motorised divisions, in which this proportion of tanks to infantry was reversed, numbered at least thirteen and probably more. (These two types of division were the exact equivalents of the German *Panzer* and, as they were later to be called, *Panzergrenadier* divisions, though the Russians were to succeed in maintaining the tank strength of their armoured regiments at a much higher level than that of the Germans).

Much, if not most, of the offensive and defensive power of the Red Army was nullified however, by the strange deployment plan which Stalin imposed on the field formations during the early summer of 1941. Russia's frontiers in that year and season were, of course, different from those which she might have had to defend two years earlier, running as they did almost everywhere well to the west of the 1939 line. The annexation of the Baltic States – Lithuania, Latvia and Estonia – had brought the Russian frontier up to the border of East Prussia in the north; the partition of Poland arrived at with Germany had advanced the central sector of the frontier almost to Warsaw; and the annexation of Bessarabia from Rumania had, in the south, carried Russian troops across the Dniester as far as the Pruth. Gratifying though the acquisition of all this territory was to Stalin, it did not make the strategic tasks of his generals any easier, for the new borders meant that the old frontier defences must now stand empty and useless many tens and in places hundreds of miles behind the military zone of operations.

An open frontier, without strong fixed defences and without formidable natural obstacles – broad rivers or lakes or high mountain ranges – demands defence in depth, by forces equipped and trained to wage mobile warfare. Large reserves, located at key centres in the communication network well behind the front, are a prerequisite of a successful defence; without such forces to hand the commander of an open frontier must live with the nightmare of an unstaunchable break-through.

It was with this nightmare that Stalin condemned his commanders

May Day 1940. Russian troops parade in Red Square

to live throughout the first half of 1941. For instead of allocating part of his forces to a strategic reserve role, he insisted on their all being deployed in the forward localities; instead of recognising that the conformation of the Russian frontier, with its many salients and re-entrants, made it uneconomic to defend every mile, he insisted on the whole length of it being manned; and instead of recognising that stretches of the frontier required less defending than others – that immediately westward of the impenetrable Pripet marshes for example, he spread his divisions out almost equidistant from each other from north to south between the Baltic and the Black Seas.

It remains therefore to enquire what could have been Stalin's motives for exposing his army to peril in so obvious a fashion as he did. They were, it has been said, 'compounded of complacency, confidence, and a form of precautionary nervousness': complacency fed by his own propaganda stories of the Red Army's invincibility; confidence that war could be avoided; and precautionary nervousness which took the form of pushing a strong screen of troops right forward so that behind it the preliminary marshalling of troops from central and eastern Russia might go undetected. To this list of motives we might add 'wishful thinking'. Stalin did not want war, stopped his ears to warnings of the dangers of war from foreign friends and would-be friends (Churchill among them), fulfilled the delivery of food and raw materials due to Germany to the letter and the minute and forbade his commanders to undertake any form of military preparation, however vital to the security of his own sector of front, which might be interpreted or represented by the Germans as an act of provocation or aggression.

In Napoleon's footsteps

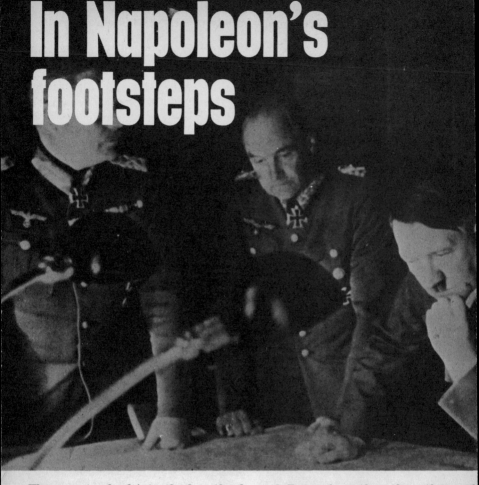

Three routes lead into the heartland of Russia. One skirts the Baltic Coast to Leningrad. The second, which Napoleon took in 1812, runs through the ancient, formerly Polish cities of Minsk and Smolensk to Moscow. The third, lying south of the Pripet Marshes but north of the Carpathian mountains, is the road from southern Poland to the black earth country of the Ukraine. Apart from the Pripet, an enormous and almost impenetrable area of fresh-water swamp and forest which divides Russia's border region strategically into distinct northern and southern halves, and apart also from the Carpathians, which protect the borders of Hungary

and Rumania rather than those of Russia, the crest line lying as it does to the westward of the international frontier, Russia is protected by no natural obstacles against invasion from Europe. For though the three traditional routes of invasion all cross broad rivers, in the enormous spaces of the Steppe the integrity of a river line is difficult to guarantee.

But to say all this is not to say that Russia is an easy country to invade. Two generals of genius, Napoleon and the Swedish King, Charles XII, threw away their reputations in Russia, and the horrors of the Grand Army's retreat from Moscow in 1812 have entered into the European folk

memory. Inefficient the Russian state might be; backward its people, undeveloped its economy, few and bad its roads (these were pre-Revolutionary judgements), but Russia was nevertheless thought of as a country virtually immune to the dangers of conquest. Schlieffen, who had made the German war plans for 1914, certainly so regarded her. He did not doubt that German soldiers could beat Russian soldiers, soundly and despite unequal numbers, but the results would never amount to better than what he called 'ordinary victories': victories, that is, in which the defeated army is neither encircled nor cornered but merely forced to vacate the battlefield. The reason why a decisive result would elude a German army in Russia, he argued, was that Russian armies were too large to be encircled and the Russian landscape devoid of obstacles against which they could be pinned. They would always slip away, therefore, and in so doing draw the invader deeper into the great inner spaces of Russia, where the climate, scorched earth and the exhaustions of the pursuit would eventually sap his strength. It was on these very reasonable grounds that Schlieffen forswore cheap eastern victories in favour of the campaign against France, tactically far more challenging but strategically less risky. This was to be his opening move in a two-front war.

Hitler inherited from Schlieffen all the problems of a two-front situation. He chose however to deal with it initially, as Bismark had done, not in military but in diplomatic terms; the outcome was the Molotov-Ribbentrop pact of 19th August 1939, by which Russia and Germany agreed not to initiate aggressive war against the other, a bargain shortly sealed by the partition between them of the territory of Poland. Hitler probably never regarded this non-aggression treaty as anything but an expedient. It is unlikely that he entertained doctrinaire motives for an attack on Russia; in almost everything, except his anti-semitism, Hitler was completely pragmatic. His common sense told him, however, that the very extent of his successes, first in defeating the Polish Army, then in overwhelming those of Belgium, Holland, France and Britain, was bound to alarm Russia, and alarm her into taking steps not to placate Germany by re-affirmation of non-aggressive policies but by increasing her military preparedness. In this judgement, as we now know, Hitler was wrong, for throughout 1940 and right up to 22nd

29

**The face of non-aggression:
Ribbentrop (left) Stalin, Molotov**

June, 1941, Stalin's policy, though it comprehended certain defensive measures, was chiefly directed to the meticulous fulfilment of the non-aggression pact, apparently in a genuinely placatory spirit. Hitler's pragmatic sense was probably accurate in warning him, however, that Stalin was buying time; and that if allowed to do so he would achieve a level of military force which, whether employed defensively or aggressively, might tax Germany beyond her strength if it came to a fight.

The continued resistance of Britain also lent emphasis to the dangers of a Russian reversal of alliances. Hitler was not so much disturbed as annoyed by Britain's persistent refusal to admit defeat, since the island kingdom was obviously incapable of intervention on the continent. But her long established tradition of maritime strategy and her skill in that field – the use in combination of her large navy and small army against the seaward flanks of Europe – made her a factor which he could never discoun[t] least of all when a principal object o[f] her strategy, when isolated, ha[d] always been, and presumably stil[l] was, to win powerful land allie[s] Russia and Britain had made commo[n] cause against Germany in the Firs[t] World War, as they had agains[t] Napoleon. For how long then coul[d] Russia resist the temptation to rene[w] those ties? Should she succumb[,] Hitler would be faced with the pros[-] pect not merely of a two but of a thre[e] front war, since Russian support fo[r] Britain would strengthen the hand o[f] the American president in his attemp[t] to bring the United States into th[e] war against Germany.

Things did not need, however, to fal[l] out in that sequence. For 'if Russi[a] drops out of the picture' as Hitle[r] explained to his service chiefs on 31s[t] July 1940, 'America too is lost fo[r] Britain, because the elimination o[f] Russia would greatly increase Japan'[s] power in the Far East: Decision[.] Russia's destruction must be made [a] part of this struggle – the soone[r]

Russia is crushed the better.' It was with this argument that Hitler justified, perhaps to himself, certainly to his subordinates, his decision to undertake studies of a blitzkrieg campaign against the Red Army.

Naturally he did not allow the preliminaries of what was still a contingency operation to interfere with the conduct of normal relations between the two dictatorships. These were regulated by the Pact of August 1939, and by subsequent agreements arrived at from time to time, notably between Ribbentrop and Molotov in Moscow in September 1939. It was under the terms of these agreements that Stalin had annexed the Baltic States in early 1940 and the Bessarabian border region of Rumania in June of that year.

Had Stalin stopped at that, Hitler could not have objected. The Russian annexation of part of Rumanian Bukovina also, outside the agreed Russian sphere of influences, gave Hitler both grounds for protest and cause for alarm. Rumania, a potential ally under the leadership of the fascist Antonescu, provided Germany with her only natural source of oil. Hitler was determined to preserve it at all costs and his Balkan diplomacy throughout the rest of the year was directed towards improving Germany's position there at the expense of Russia's. Hungary was bribed with a share of Rumanian territory, Rumania was placated by the despatch of German troops to guard her oilfields (a guarantee against further Russian annexation) and Russia was given to understand that these moves were designed to repel any *British* intervention in the area. Stalin nevertheless took fright at these initiatives, as also at Italy's invasion of Greece in late October (abortive, as it was to turn out), and in mid-November sent Molotov to Berlin to beard Hitler and extract concrete assurances of good-neighbourliness from him. This Molotov failed to do; had he known that Hitler was planning a rapid Balkan campaign for the coming spring (Operation Marita) he would have gone home in even greater disquiet over the Balkan situation. Had he guessed to what stage of planning the Germans had brought Operation Barbarossa, the code name under which the projected invasion of Russia was now known, he might not have dared to return, so completely did that plan spell the ruin of his diplomacy.

Hitler probably first breathed his intention to attack Russia to General Halder, the Chief of the Army High Command (OKH), on 2nd July 1940 (the same day as he issued his operation order for 'Sealion', the invasion of Britain.) Hitler was never very serious in his intention of attacking England, perhaps because he suspected the inability of the Luftwaffe to overcome Fighter Command, perhaps because he had already mentally plumped for Russia. It was on plans for Russia that he henceforth concentrated. The original planning brief was given to the head of the operations section of his own personal staff, OKW, General Jodl (who was to hang at Nuremberg for his part in 'preparing and waging aggressive war'). He in turn explained it to his subordinates on 19th July, rousing them thereby to an explosion of disbelief. Hitler, however, also commissioned Halder to prepare plans, an order which the Army Chief of Staff delegated to General Marcks. Marcks' plan, presented on 5th August 1940, was to lay down the broad guidelines which the final invasion plan would follow.

He made the assumption that the Russians would not attack the Germans, though it would be convenient if they did (Schlieffen had made the same judgement about the French before 1914, wrongly as it turned out), and that the Wehrmacht would enjoy a small superiority in numbers of men, a distinct superiority in numbers of armoured units and some superiority in quality of equipment. Making allowances for the need to maintain garrisons in the occupied countries Marcks calculated that Germany would be able to field 110 infantry, 24 panzer and 12 motorised divisions against 96 Russian infantry divisions (the Russians called them 'rifle' divisions), 23 cavalry divisions and 28 armoured brigades (the Germans as yet knew nothing of Timoshenko's re-establishment of mechanised corps and divisions). Marcks would allocate the bulk of the German divisions to two central Army Groups, the one operating south eastward towards Kiev, capital of the Ukraine, and the other due east from Poland towards Moscow, along the great lateral highway, running through Minsk and Smolensk, which Napoleon and the Grand Army had taken in 1812. There were to be two subsidiary operations, the first an advance on Leningrad from the same base of operations as the northern-most of the central army groups, the other an advance on Kiev by a German-Rumanian force operating across annexed Bessarabia. The central Army Groups, however, were those which would have to make the plan work; once they had achieved their initial objectives – Moscow and Kiev respectively, they were to advance rapidly on each other and complete the encirclement of Russian troops to their west. This last objective was the principal aim of Marcks' plan. The Red Army was to be surrounded and destroyed between the rivers Dvina and Dnieper, and all within the space of nine to seventeen weeks.

This plan, though much amended later, laid down the fundamentals of German strategy for Barbarossa, in particular that of the German *Army* (as we shall see, the Army's strategic views and Hitler's came later to differ, with noteworthy results). The Marcks plan was nevertheless as yet a planning study rather than an operational directive, and, while work continued on the problems it had isolated, the High Command of the Wehrmacht (OKW), Hitler's personal plannin[g] and operations staff, turned to th[e] practical preparations. The first tas[k] was to effect the transfer of majo[r] forces from the western to the easter[n] theatre, amounting in all to 35 divi[-] sions, by 24th October 1940. Thi[s] gigantic redeployment of a whol[e] Army Group, one of the three whic[h] had been unleashed against the wes[-] tern allies in May, was explained t[o] interested parties, who certainly in[-] cluded the Russians, as being designe[d] to provide the divisions involved wit[h] more expansive training areas tha[n] could be found in the West, while als[o] removing them from the danger o[f] British air attack. In fact, som[e] redisposition of force between Franc[e] and Poland was perfectly explicable i[n] military terms, for with three Arm[y] Groups – both the bulk and flower o[f] her land forces – assigned to the west[,] Germany's strategic posture was badl[y] out of balance.

Under the Codename of *Aufbau Os[t]* these preliminaries were satis[-] factorily carried through by OKW. A[t] the same time its operations sectio[n] was preparing a strategic appreciatio[n] of the invasion problem, which it wa[s] to present to Hitler. The conclusion[s] it arrived at were different from thos[e] of OKH: instead of recommending that the major effort be made along the Minsk-Smolensk axis, the road t[o] Moscow, OKW felt that the invading German army should be divided into three more or less equal groups, directed respectively against Lenin-grad in the north, and Kiev in the south, as well as against Moscow in the centre. This might have seemed no more than a technical difference of treatment by the two staffs, had not the thinking of OKW also been that its three groups should 'keep station' with each other in line abreast. This suggestion, though guarding against certain obvious risks, would almost certainly lead to the German army achieving nothing more than those 'ordinary' victories which Schlieffen had been so reluctant to embark upon

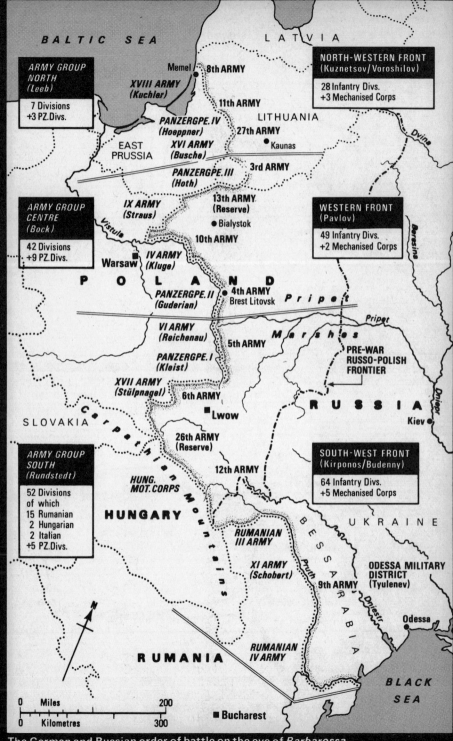

The German and Russian order of battle on the eve of *Barbarossa*

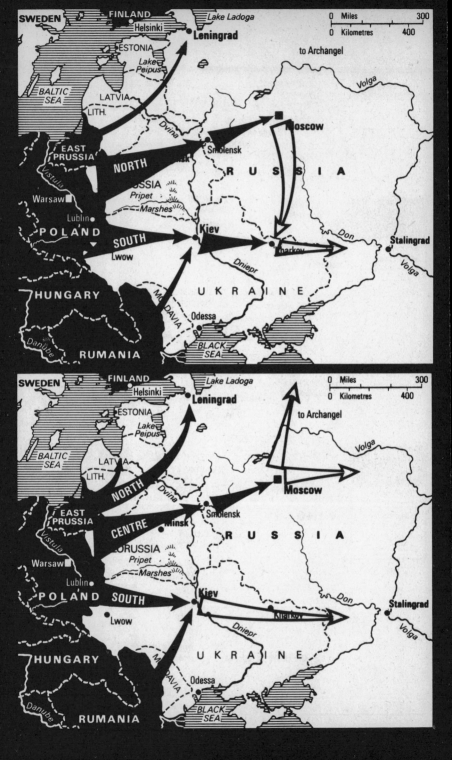

Above left: Marcks Plan: heavy thrusts towards Moscow and Kiev, with the Baltic and Black Sea flanks left to much lighter forces. *Left:* OKH Plan: Leningrad becomes a third primary objective, while the Moscow thrust is strengthened at the expense of the drive on Kiev. *Above:* Hitler's variant, 'Barbarossa': the capture of Leningrad is stipulated as essential before the subsequent – and conclusive – drive on Moscow

Marcks, author of the Army's plan for Barbarossa

Halder, Chief of the Army General Staff

Ritter von Leeb, Commander of Army Group North

Von Bock, the Primadonna of Army Group Centre

The Black Knight: Rundstedt, Commander of Army Group South

The Waffen-SS on the road to Greece, April 1941

German armour and artillery in the mountains of Yugoslavia, 1941

thirty years earlier.

Meanwhile the Army High Command (OKH) had spent the autumn refining the broad guidelines laid down by Marcks and at the end of November subjected the conclusions to which it had come to the rigorous logic of a large-scale war game, one of the most venerated methods of finalising plans in the German army. Its results, encapsulated in an address given by Halder, the Army Chief of Staff, to an audience which included Hitler, seemed to recommend a marriage between elements both of the original OKH and the later OKW plans: that is to say, an advance by three rather than two army groups but with the emphasis on the effort towards Moscow. The central passage of Halder's address ran as follows:

'The most important Russian armament centres lie in the Ukraine, in Moscow and in Leningrad. The entire operational area is split into two halves, to the north and south, by the Pripet Marshes; in the southern half, the road network is poor, to the north road and rail links are better in the Warsaw-Moscow area. This northern sector is also more heavily manned with Soviet troops, massed towards the Soviet-German demarcation line (bisecting occupied Poland). The Dnieper and the Dvina are the most easterly lines the Russians must defend; pulling back any further uncovers their industrial regions. The German intention must be to prevent any concentrated build up of resistance to the west of those rivers by pushing in armoured wedges.

'A particularly powerful assault force must strike from Warsaw in the direction of Moscow. Of the three proposed Army Groups, the northern would form its focal point on Leningrad, the southern on Kiev, and from the latter Army Group one army would advance from Labun, a second from Lemberg (Lwow) and a third from Rumania. The target for the entire operation would be the Volga and the region of Archangel: 105 infantry and 32 panzer and motorised divisions would be employed, of which strong elements (two armies) would follow initially in the second wave.'

This statement formed the basis on which the two staffs, OKH and OKW, jointly prepared the final directive. It was presented to Hitler on 17th December 1940 and issued in only nine copies, all super-secret, the following day. Overnight, however, Hitler had amended the objects and objectives laid down by his military advisors, and in no marginal way. The division of force between the three Army Groups remained intact, as did their initial tasks. As soon, however, as the Russian armies defending White Russia (Belorussia – that region east of Poland, and north of the Pripet) had been destroyed, strong elements of Army Group Centre were to be detached to assist Army Group North to secure the Baltic coast and Leningrad. Not until that operation had been completed was the advance on Moscow – the manoeuvre which OKH had always regarded as decisive – to be undertaken.

Here was the crucial ingredient of *Operation Barbarossa*, as Hitler now officially chose to codename his Operational Directive No 21. It contained, however, much besides. North Russian was to be invaded by a mountain army operating out of Finland, probably in co-operation with the Finnish army. The Rumanian army, now effectively under German control, was to provide sizeable contingents to flank Army Group South's advance towards Kiev. The eventual boundary of the German advance was fixed on the Volga-Archangel line, beyond which the 'last surviving industrial area of Russia in the Urals can then if necessary be eliminated by the Luftwaffe'.

The strengths of the three Army Groups were now fixed. Army Group North was to consist of the Sixteenth

A German MG-34 team picks its way across the Drava into Yugoslavia, April 1941

38

German self-propelled guns advance in the Balkans

and Eighteenth Armies of eighteen infantry divisions, and the First Panzergruppe, or Panzer Army as it would later be called; it counted three panzer and three motorised divisions on its strength, and was commanded by General Hoeppner. The Army Group Commander was Field-Marshal Ritter von Leeb.

Army Group Centre, commanded by Field-Marshal von Bock, consisted of the Fourth and Ninth Armies, together with twenty-four infantry divisions. Its order of battle was completed by the Second and Third Panzergruppen, commanded by Guderian, the great tank theorist, and Hoth. Between them they shared seven panzer and seven motorised divisions.

Army Group South, commanded by Field-Marshal von Runstedt, the 'Black Knight of the German Army', consisted of the Sixth, Eleventh and Seventeenth Armies, the Third and Fourth Rumanian Armies and Kleist's First Panzergruppe. The Eleventh and the two Rumanian Armies were detached from the main body, which was to concentrate east of the Lublin and Cracow, being aligned along the river Pruth in the far south. Runstedt's total force amounted to thirty-one divisions, of which five were panzer and three motorised. Comparatively speaking, it was therefore much the weakest in armour.

All the panzer divisions were weaker in tanks than they had been in 1939. This was due to the formation of a whole new series of panzer divisions, done by withdrawing cadres from those already existing. The results were not wholly detrimental, for the original tank strength in the panzer divisions – nearly 400 – was certainly too high and too many of the tanks (Mark II and even Mark I) too weak. Fewer but heavier tanks (Mark IIIs and Mark IVs) made a better complement, when balanced against a rather

41

Left: The Germans find a way round Greece, 1941. *Below:* Instant collaboration, Salonika, 1941

larger proportion of infantry. The new establishment of a panzer division in 1941, therefore, stood at: one tank regiment of two (sometimes three) *Abteilungen*, with 150–200 tanks; two motorised Rifle (*Schützen*) regiments (soon to be called Panzer Grenadiers) of two battalions each, whose soldiers were carried in armoured half-tracks or similar vehicles; and a motor-cycle reconnaissance battalion. The artillery, also fully motorised, comprised two field, one medium and one anti-tank regiment. Divisional Headquarters controlled an armoured car reconnaissance battalion and a small flight of spotter aircraft. The motorised infantry divisions were on a similar scale of organisation, though they lacked the tank element and had an additional rifle regiment; the function of these divisions was to keep pace with the panzers and to supplement their infantry in the deliberate attack, or whenever there was much mopping-up to be done of isolated pockets of resistance.

The quantity of mechanical transport possessed by both sorts of formation set them quite apart from the ordinary infantry divisions. The latter's scales of equipment were scarcely, if at all, different from those of the Kaiser's infantry which had marched to war in 1914. Horsedrawn artillery batteries and first-line transport echelons, plodding battalions – these were not the formations with which the Germans would win battles of encirclement. As the events of 1940 in France had shown, however, it was the speed attained by the armour spearheads which counted in the new warfare – warfare German-style. As long as the infantry could guarantee to maintain a steady thirty or forty kilometres a day, the panzers could take the risk of putting themselves as much as a hundred kilometres into the blue. They had then only to hang on

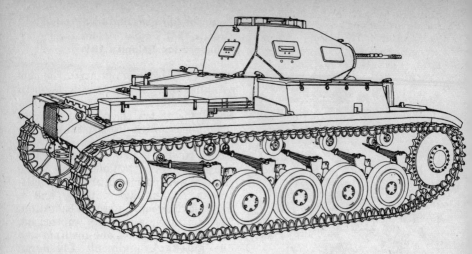

Panzerkampfwagen II Ausf 'F' (Sd KFZ 121). Produced in 1940. *Crew:* 3 men.
Weight: 9.5 tons. *Armament:* One 2cm Kw.K 30 and coaxial 7.92mm MG 34. *Rounds
carried:* 2cm – 180, 7.92mm – 2550. *Engine:* 140 HP Maybach HL 62 TR. *Speed:* Road
30mph, c/c 12mph. *Overall length:* 14 feet 9 inches. *Overall width:* 7 feet 4 inches
Overall height: 6 feet 6 inches. The quarter-elliptic leaf suspension was similar to
that fitted to models A, B, C but an entirely new hull was constructed for this
version and the armour thickness increased

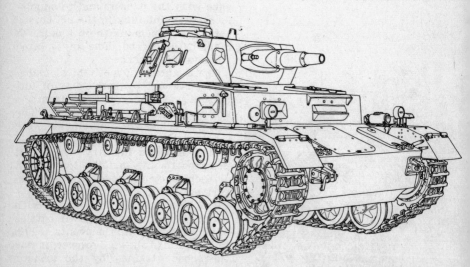

Panzerkampfwagen IV Ausf 'C'. *Weight:* 20 tons. *Crew:* 5 men. *Armament:* Main
gun 7.5cm Kw.K (L/24), coaxial 7.92mm machine gun. *Rounds carried:* 7.5cm – 80,
7.92mm – 2,700. *Engine:* 300 HP Maybach HL 120 TRM. *Maximum speed:* Road
40 kph, c/c 20 kph. *Overall length:* 587cm. *Overall width:* 285cm. *Overall height:*
259cm. This model was not fitted with a hull machine gun, but was provided with a
pistol port shown on the extreme left of the front plate. Note the single hatch door,
fitted in each side of the turret twin hatch doors appeared on models F onwards
The 7.5cm gun is mounted in an internal gun mantlet

Panzerkampfwagen III Ausf 'F'. *Weight*: 20.3 tons. *Crew*: 5 men. *Armament*: Main gun 5 cm Kw.K (L/42), coaxial 7.92mm machine gun, hull 7.92mm machine gun *Rounds carried*: 5cm – 99, 7.92mm – 2600. *Engine*: 300 HP Maybach HL 120 TRM *Maximum speed*: Road 40 kph, c/c 18 kph. *Overall length*: 541cm. *Overall width*: 292cm. *Overall height*: 244cm

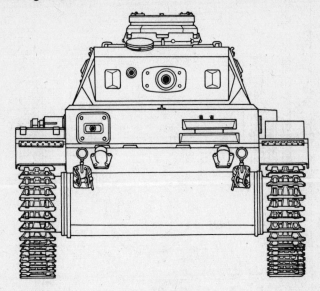

Front view: shows drivers visor on right, hull machine gun on left, two ventilator cowls on glacis plate. Two vision ports for loader and gunner are shown on the turret gun mantlet

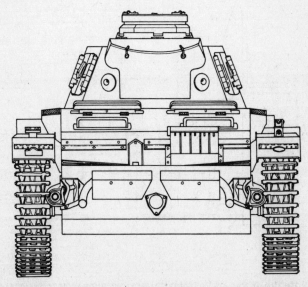

Rear view: shows rack containing five smoke generators, these were released by means of a rod controlled from turret.

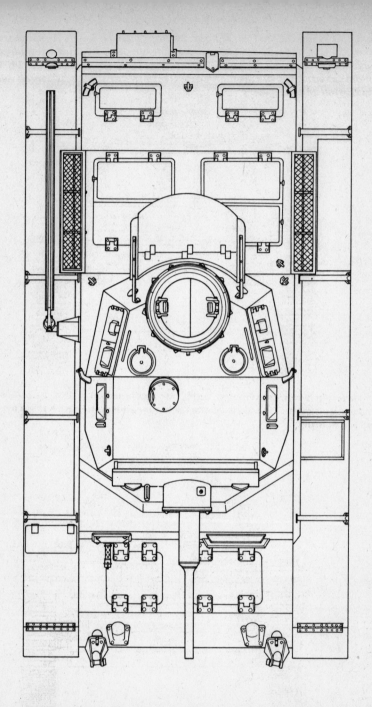

Top view : **Note the driver and wireless operators access hatches in the top of the front superstructure, and the engine hatches at the rear. A wireless aerial is shown at the right rear corner**

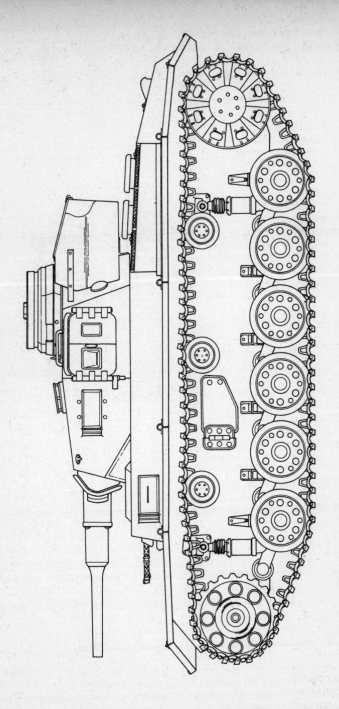

Side view : Note escape hatch in hull side. This vehicle is fitted with the early type of commanders cupola with five vision ports, and with stowage box ar rear of turret. This type of driving sprocket and idler wheel was also used on models E and G

for two to three days, and the slower moving infantry would be up with them.

The concentration of this vast collection of infantry and mechanised divisions for Barbarossa was scheduled to be completed by 15th May. They were to move eastward in four waves. The first, by the time the Barbarossa directive was issued, was already in place. The second was to arrive by mid-March, the third by mid-April, and the fourth by late April. By that last stage, it would no longer be possible to disguise the extent of the deployment. But before the planned concentration could be completed, the smooth development of Hitler's plans for the eastern theatre of operations was rudely interrupted by events in the Balkans. In late March, a group of nationalist and anti-Nazi officers of the Yugoslav army, led by General Merkovitch, overthrew the Regency of Prince Paul, a strong pro-Nazi, and renounced his signature of the Tripartite Pact, which bound their country to Germany, Italy and Japan. Hitler, who had begun to feel a scornful impatience at the Italians' lack of success in their private war with Greece, now decided that he must intervene directly and decisively in the Balkans. Troops which had been assigned to Barbarossa were regrouped and re-aligned. A new directive was issued; and on 6th April the Balkan campaign began.

It was swiftly finished: the Yugoslavs capitulated on 17th April; The Greek armies fighting on the Albanian front capitulated on 20th April; the Greek government accepted defeat four days later and on the same day the British expeditionary force, which Churchill had sent to the Greeks' assistance as soon as the Germans had intervened, started its own withdrawal, in part via Crete. That island fell into German hands, as the result of a brilliant but extremely costly airborne operation, on 26th May.

This Balkan campaign did not however have for its outcome merely

the passage of more territory into German hands. That – given particularly the strategic significance of the territory seized – was important enough. But what was of greater, as things were to turn out, of crucial significance, was the delay the campaign imposed on the launching of Barbarossa. Originally planned for 15th May, it was not now to being until mid-June – a delay of five weeks – weeks which, as Hitler and the world were later to recognise, perhaps spelt the difference between success and failure for the German army in Russia. Five weeks is a very big bite out of the Russian summer.

Hitler himself, though irritated by the delay imposed by the Balkan campaign – initially, indeed, driven into a frenzy of rage by Yugoslavia's 'perfidy' – was in no way shaken by it from his resolve to proceed. Barbarossa, however pragmatically he had arrived at the decision to launch it,

German paratroopers assault a
British position on Crete, May 1941

had now become an obsession with him. The codename – the nickname of a German emperor who had led his armies on a Crusade against the pagan Slavs in the 12th Century – betrays the historical role in which he had cast himself. And the mood in which he was preparing to play it was a pitiless and extortionate one. He had revealed it to his commanders of the armed services in a speech to them during March:

'The war against Russia,' he had said, 'will be such that it cannot be conducted in a knightly fashion: the struggle is one of ideologies and racial differences and will have to be conducted with unprecedented, unmerciful and unrelenting harshness. All officers will have to rid themselves of obsolete ideologies. I know that the necessity for such means of making war is beyond the comprehension of you generals but . . . I insist absolutely that my orders be executed without contradiction. The commissars are the bearers of ideologies directly opposed to National Socialism. Therefore the commissars will be liquidated. German soldiers guilty of breaking international law . . . will be excused. Russia has not participated in the Hague Convention and therefore has no rights under it.'

For many in the German army, these were intolerable sentiments, but none would protest directly and most, as things turned out, would obey orders issued in this spirit. For officials of the SS, the Party or the State who were to be concerned with the administration and exploitation of captured Russian territory, Hitler's speech merely made explicit the policies which they had been preparing to implement in detail for some time already. Russia, under their hands, was to die the death of a thousand cuts.

The great breakthrough

The short summer night of 21st/22nd June 1941 passed quietly on the whole length of Russia's frontier with western Europe. The Berlin-Moscow express crossed at the scheduled time. The customs posts remained open.

At 3.30 an intense barrage descended. The flimsy Russian forward defences disappeared under a curtain of smoke. Behind it the leading mass of German infantry and armour moved to the attack. One Russian advanced headquarters signalled higher command, 'We are being fired on. What shall we do?' 'You must be mad', was the reply, 'And why is your signal not in code?'

Contrary to general belief, however, the Russians were not taken wholly by surprise on 22nd June: or, more accurately, the highest echelons were not. Timoshenko, presumably acting with Stalin's approval, actually issued an alert to the staffs of the military districts, warning them of the likelihood of a German dawn attack on the coming day and ordering them to stand-to their units.

This warning came far too late for effective measures to be taken against the German onset. Indeed most of the Russian formations deployed forward received no warning at all of the assault and were overwhelmed in their positions. This was not surprising. The frontier defences, which the Red Army had of course occupied only

A reconnaissance battalion of
Panzergruppe 2 passes Guderian,
July 1942

since September 1939 (and on the southern sector, in the former Rumanian provinces only since June 1940), were organised neither strongly nor in depth. Strength and depth – plus a large mobile counter-attack reserve – are essential in parrying an armoured thrust. Russia possessed none of these things. The Stalin line, though impressively fortified along some stretches, lay too far behind the post-1939 frontier to lend it strength, while the deployment Stalin had ordained for the Red Army was almost completely linear. Wherever units were echeloned back in any depth, however, it seems that during the earliest days the Russian high command sent them forward at once to stem the flood. Command decisions of this sort would play directly into the Germans' hands.

German strategy on the central front, along the Minsk-Smolensk road to Moscow, was simple. It was to encircle as much of the Russian army defending the area as possible, cutting off its line of retreat eastward over the Dwina and Dnieper rivers, and there to hack or hug it to death. Thereafter Army Group Centre was to secure the 'Land Bridge' between the headwaters of the Dwina and the Dnieper (which flow respectively into the Baltic and Black Seas) and pass across it towards Moscow.

The first stage of Army Group Centre's attack passed off with almost unnerving success. Its supporting contingent of the Luftwaffe, Luftflotte (Airfleet) 2, destroyed vast numbers of the Red Air Forces' planes on the ground and, when it encountered opposition in the air, drove it from the sky with heavy loss. Against planes and pilots of the quality and experience of the Luftwaffe, the Russians, whose new generation of modern fighters were only just coming into service, were no match. On the ground their infantry, always brave, lacked the weapons to resist the penetration of strong panzer columns; their anti-tank rifles could not pierce the armour of a Mark III, let alone that of the Mark IV, and their 47mm anti-tank gun – an excellent weapon which the Germans themselves would later adopt enthusiastically – was not yet distributed in quantity. Thus it was that Army Group Centre's divisions, though having to open their operations with the assault crossing of a river – the Niemen on the northern, the Bug on the southern sector of the front – quite easily found a footing on the far bank and made ground quickly. Brest-Litovsk, the frontier fortress at which the Germans had dictated peace to the

51

Above: Assault river crossing. *Left:* A
column of Mark IV Panzers

Bolsheviks twenty-three years before,
held out for nearly a week. It did not,
however, hold up the advance, even
though it commanded an important
crossing over the Bug, since the
Germans merely left a division to mask
it (rather as they had done at Mau-
beuge on their way to the Marne in
1914), while building alternative crossings to its south.

This breakthrough was very dangerous to the Russians opposite Army
Group Centre – they formed the Third,
Fourth, Tenth and Thirteenth Armies
– since the Russian frontier – the post-
1939 frontier which Stalin had insisted
they should man closely along its
whole length – bent westwards at that
point, running into a great salient,
called the Bialystok salient, whose
other face was formed by the German
positions in East Prussia. When
matched by a similar breakthrough by
the Germans from East Prussia itself,
that at Brest-Litovsk threatened the

whole Russian army in Army Group
Centre's zone of operations with
encirclement.

Von Bock's assessment of the results
of the first two days of the battle led
him to believe that, in order to escape
from this impending threat of
encirclement, the Russian troops
opposite, perhaps under orders from
the High Command, were abandoning
their positions and fleeing eastwards
with the intention of re-establishing
their defences on the Dwina-Dnieper.
He accordingly put it to the Army High
Command (OKH) that the Panzergruppen, in particular Hoth's Panzergruppe 3, should abandon its mission
to close the pincers around Minsk –
200 miles from their start lines – and
should press on directly for Smolensk
on the Dnieper, another 125 miles further on. But OKH, fearing the isolation
of the Panzergruppe it it should fall in
such a dash – and isolation leads to
destruction in blitzkrieg – insisted
that he stick to the original directive:
the closure of the pincers first around
Minsk, only later round Smolensk.

Left: Into the steppe. *Below:left:*
Waiting to advance, June 30th 1941

Panzergruppe 3 accordingly began
its inward turn on 24th June.

It now became apparent that the
Russians who had been seen fleeing
were not intent upon a strategic
withdrawal but had merely abandoned
untenable positions. Those new positions to which their flight carried
them, between the constricting arms
of the Panzergruppen and the
marching divisions of Fourth and
Ninth Armies, proved no healthier.

The Russians could not outrun the
German armoured columns which,
pressing on at speeds of fifty miles a
day or more, were probably the fastest
military formations in the world at
that date. OKH's fears, however, that
if allowed to press on without regard
for their rearward communications,
the panzers would dangerously over-
extend themselves, now began to be
proved correct. For the entrapped
Russians, fighting desperately, were
finding the weak spots in the arms of
the pincer, particularly that formed
by Guderian's Panzergruppe 2, and
were breaking out south-eastwards. It
was a development which OKH particularly disliked, for the escaping
formations would make naturally for
the marshes of the Pripet where,
lurking in those impenetrable fast-
nesses, they were likely to offer a
serious threat to the German supply
echelons when they came to pass that
way later.

On 25th June, therefore, in the light
of both these dangers – the isolation of
units of Panzergruppe 2 and the
generation of a 'stay behind' threat to
the army's rear, OKH ordered the
infantry divisions of Fourth and Ninth
Armies to engage the enemy more
closely. The object of this order was to
bring about by military means what,
in the fighting with the French in 1940,
had been achieved by moral effect –
the destruction of the enemy's capacity to resist. Surrounded Russian
soldiers did not behave like French

oldiers in a similar circumstance. All too often they fought on and had to be killed before the ground they held could be secured.

Thus it came about that by 25th June Army Group Centre found itself fighting no less than three battles of encirclement: one – the least in scale – around the fortress of Brest-Litowsk; one around Biaylstok, where six Russian divisions had been surrounded in the initial onrush; and one around Volkovysk, where another six divisions had been surrounded by 25th June.

By 29th June, the Army Group was fighting yet another encirclement battle; that to reduce a large pocket just to the westward of Minsk into which some fifteen divisions, either refugees from the frontier or reinforcements from within Russia, had been corralled. The following day the reduction of the Bialystok and Volkovysk pockets had advanced so far that considerable drafts could be safely made on the infantry strength of the cordons surrounding them and those sent to fill in the gaps in the armoured chain around the Minsk pocket.

It was not to be until 9th July, however, that the Minsk pocket finally succumbed to German pressure, for their infantry had far to come to the panzers' assistance and over the most scanty and atrocious road network.

Orders for the next stage had been issued by OKH on 1st July, together with a directive subordinating both Hoth's and Guderian's Panzergruppen to Kluge who, handing over his former command, now renumbered Second Army, to General von Weichs, became commander of the Fourth Panzer Army. The first orders he received in his new appointment were to prepare his army to 'break through in the direction of Moscow'. Panzergruppe 2 was accordingly to force a crossing of the Dnieper south of Smolensk, to

follow the line of the Minsk-Moscow motorway (alas for panzer commanders with visions of driving their tanks down an autobahn: much of it as yet consisted only of a dirt surface) and to seize the Yelna heights at the bend of the River Desna. Panzergruppe 3, on the northern flank, was to remain on its present axis and proceed along the upper Dvina as far as Vitebsk, where it was to break across and capture ground north of Smolensk. The infantry armies, Second (ex Fourth) and Ninth, were to press their efforts to keep up as closely as they could with the armoured spearheads. Luftwaffe support was to remain as previously arranged, Fliegerkorps II supporting the armies in the south, Fliegerkorps VIII those in the northern arm of the pincers.

The operation began at once on 3rd July, before the infantry of the two marching armies of the Army Group had had time to finish quelling the last Russian resistance in the Minsk pocket. The advance on Smolensk was perforce organised initially as an armoured operation.

Almost immediately it encountered heavier opposition than any so far. Panzergruppe 2 was held up when attempting to make a crossing of the Beresina near Borisov on the main Minsk-Smolensk road. Subsidiary crossings at Rogachev on the Dnieper and Polotsk on the Dvina did not provide, at least to the thinking of Army Group Centre's staff, acceptable alternative axes of advance. This situation posed, in a most urgent form, the problem, inherent in blitzkrieg operations, of whether to accept delay and wait for the infantry to catch up, or to commit the armour to an infantry-style assault on the enemy's defended position. Both were unsatisfactory solutions: awaiting the infantry entailed loss of time, time in which the enemy could be guaranteed to improve his positions and summon reserves; but an infantry style assault meant exposing the armour and the highly trained motorised

The Swastika rises over Brest-Litovsk, 9th July 1941

Above left: An assault pioneer platoon crosses the Bug at Litonitz, 22nd June 1941. Left: Minsk, after bombing by the Luftwaffe. Above: Motorised column advances through the ruins of Minsk

units (panzer grenadiers, as they were soon to be called) to heavy losses, which could not easily be made good.

Bock decided to risk accepting losses, but rightly decided to concentrate the armour of Panzergruppe 2 before attempting the stroke. It was to be shifted to the Mogilev sector, on the Dnieper, and strike towards Smolensk, on secondary roads and across country. The quality of resistance put up by the Russian defenders of this vital river line was to make this a mission more easily defined than accomplished: not until 10th July, a week after the operation had begun, did units of Panzergruppe 2 manage to find footholes on the far shore.

By then, however, Panzergruppe 3 had won an important breakthrough

on the northern route to Smolensk, having destroyed the Russian defences of the Dvina and established a major bridgehead at Vitebsk. So promising did this development appear to Bock that he momentarily considered marching a major part of Panzergruppe 2 across country to join in the exploitation from this point. Reports of bad going deterred him from issuing the necessary orders, however, and by the time the ground had dried out, Guderian's panzers had won their own bridgehead near Mogilev.

Very hard fighting on both the northern and southern bridgeheads between 11th and 13th July led at last to the true breakthrough for which Bock, Hoth and Guderian had been so anxious. Hoth's Panzergruppe 3 was particularly quick away from the river and was able to put a division across the Smolensk-Moscow road on 15th July. On the following day it sent a division into the city and captured it outright, to its own surprise as much as the defenders'. When its fellow

Panzergruppe's spearheads arrived at Yelna, fifty miles south-east of Smolensk on 17th July, the new pocket was almost complete. Dotted about inside it were groups of Russian divisions – six-seven near Mogilev, three-four near Vitebsk and a large body, twelve-fourteen strong east of Smolensk. None could now offer a serious threat to the Germans, since their munitions had run low and they were almost cut off from sources of resupply, but they had to be prevented from breaking-out and forced into surrender without delay.

As before, it was to the infantry of

Russian prisoners taken at Smolensk

Second and Ninth Armies that the bulk of the work should have properly fallen, but their divisions were at distances of anything up to 200 miles behind the leading armour at this stage of the battle in mid-July and unable to get up any faster than their feet would carry them: twenty miles a day was as much as they could be asked to do. As a result the hastily drawn cordons of tanks, half-tracks and dismounted panzer grenadiers were not able to prevent parties of Russian soldiers slipping through to the east. And at one point, in the valley of the Dnieper, a wide stretch of terrain had to be left completely unguarded, so taxed was

Guderian by calls on his resources elsewhere. Through this particular gap quite important numbers of Russians, many still moving as formed units, were able to break out – if not to safety, for nowhere in western Russia could be called safe in the summer of 1941 – then at least to fight again another day. It was not until 27th July that a watertight barrier could be drawn around the whole pocket and not until 5th August that all Russian resistance within it was brought to a standstill.

Part of the reason was that the Dnieper gap had been used during the time that it remained open not wholly as a means of escape but also, as the Germans were slow in detecting, as a channel of reinforcement and re-supply. That discovery lent definition to an intelligence picture which hinted at a far more resolute and adaptive Russian response to the challenge of blitzkrieg than the Germans had encountered in the west. Faced by the German onslaught, and the palpable collapse, almost everywhere within the first few hours, of their frontier defences – to say nothing of the collapse of their claims for those defences' impregnability and of the invincibility of the Red Army – the Russian leadership had nevertheless kept its collective head. An executive war council (GOKO) had been set up on

Molotov

Germans burn out partisans, July 1941

Beria, chief of Stalin's secret police

Prisoners taken in the Smolensk encirclement

Above: German (ex-Czech) 35 (t) tank (foreground) and Panzer Mark IIIs
Below: The Luftwaffe caught much of the Red Air Force on the ground.
1-16 fighters (left) and PE-2 bomber (foreground)

23rd June, consisting of Stalin, Voro-shilov (Commissar for Defence), Beria (Head of the NKVD, the Secret State Police), Molotov (Commissar for Foreign Affairs) and Malenkov (Stalin's Deputy in the Party machine). Directly subordinate to this State Defence Committee there was established an operational military staff, the Stavka, which, when re-organised on 10th July, comprised as members Stalin, Molotov, and Voro-shilov from the Party side and, from the Army, Timoshenko, Budenny, Shaposhnikov, Chief of the General Staff, and Zhukov, the victor of the battle of Kholkin-Gol against the Japanese in 1939. This mixed Party-Army composition of the Stavka was not merely conventional communist practice: it also reflected the re-imposition of direct political control over the exercise of military com-mand. 'Dual Command' (ie the sharing of responsibility between officer and commissar) was reintroduced into the Red Army on 16th July.

Another re-introduction, though from an older political tradition, was the execution of unsuccessful (offi-cially characterised as 'guilty') generals: the commander of the Western Front, General Pavlov, whose lines had resisted so briefly the onset of Army Group Centre, was shot early in July, together with his Chief of Staff and Chief Signals Officer. They were not to be the last victims, nor would all be so high-ranking: units of the NKVD – 'rear security detach-ments' – were posted behind the whole Russian line of battle in order to inter-cept and remonstrate with any – in-dividuals or formed units – who left it unordered.

Besides providing for the exercise of authority at the highest and lowest levels, Stalin and the Stavka also arranged, on 10th July, for a more realistic command structure in the field. Three new Fronts were set up (a Russian Front is equivalent to a wes-tern Army Group), with boundaries approximately similar to those of the three German Army Groups opposite. Army Group South (Runstedt) was now to be faced by the South-Western Front, under Marshal Budenny, intel-lectually no match for Runstedt but a charismatic figure from the heroic age of the Red Army in the Civil War; as his political commissar Stalin ap-pointed Nikita Krushchev, a trusted subordinate and former agent of collectivisation in the Ukraine. Army Group Centre (Bock) was now to be opposed by a new Western Front, under Timoshenko, and Army Group North by a North-Western Front under the nominal command of Voroshilov.

Reorganisation below, resolution above, provided however no answer to Russia's most pressing problem; want of trained manpower and first-class equipment at the front. Her losses, by mid-July, had reached staggering proportions. Of her air force, over 3,000 planes had been destroyed, most with-in the first five days, and that was a conservative figure: others went as high as 6,000, which represented vir-tually the whole of Russia's first-line air strength. Her losses on land had been even greater: of 164 Red divisions identified, OKH reckoned on 8th July to have destroyed eighty-nine, or over half. As a running check, which added authenticity to this estimate, Army Group Centre was able to show that it had taken 300,000 prisoners, 2,500 tanks and 1,400 guns, in the process virtually destroying four Soviet Armies. In the battle of the Smolensk pocket, just beginning at the time Stalin reorganised his High Command, Army Group Centre was to take another 310,000 prisoners, 3,200 tanks and 3,100 guns. Much of the equipment was admittedly second rate – few of the new T-34s or KV-Is had yet come into service – but very little remained in the arsenals to make good such losses. As for the losses of men, these could be replaced only by drafts from the reserves or from the half-trained ranks of the *Osoaviakhim;* destroyed formations were replaced by the creation of units of *Opolchenie,* the

Left: The nests of resistance are in flames and the march continues.
Below: German troops advance past burning buildings

'people's militia'.

Yet despite the disasters, and the evident incompetence of much of the military machine, there were few reports of voluntary surrenders on any large-scale. Stalin's appeal to fight a 'Patriotic War' had struck a responsive chord in this people of traditionally deep attachment to their motherland – Russian soldiers surrendered when they had to, and sometimes this meant in very large numbers. But the bulk of German reports of the campaign, both official and personal, emphasise rather their stubborn refusal to lay down their arms unless completely surrounded and out of ammunition.

But the state of Russian morale was not uppermost in German minds at this moment. Dazzled by the sheer material scale of the victory on the central front, they were calculating its results and contemplating the future. For it was not only on the front of Army Group Centre that results had been achieved. Both other Army Groups had won much ground and inflicted serious defeats on the enemy which opposed them.

Army Group North, weakest of the three with only twenty infantry divisions and a single Panzergruppe, No 4 under Hoepner, had been given Leningrad as its objective in the Barbarossa directive; it was also to secure the coast of the Gulf of Finland and, most important, it was to destroy the Russian forces in its path. Since the total opposition to the attack of Panzergruppe 4 offered by the Russians on 22nd July was that of a single rifle division, occupying a front of forty miles, its swift penetration of the frontier defences was made very easy. Marching in three columns – Eighteenth Army along the coast, Panzergruppe 4 in the centre, Sixteenth Army on the right, flanking the

northernmost divisions of Army Group Centre, it passed quickly into Lithuania and by 30th June had secured bridgeheads over the Dvina, along which the Stalin Line was supposed to run. Racing on through it, the Panzergruppe, after one or two false turns, arrived on 4th July at Ostrov, across the pre-1939 Russian frontier with Latvia. Ten days later, having by-passed whatever Russian concentrations stood in its way XLI Corps of Panzergruppe 4 stood on the line of the Luga, last important river obstacle before Leningrad and only sixty miles from the city.

Army Group South, commanded by the most orthodox but also perhaps personally the most impressive of all the senior German officers of the Ostheer, Field-Marshal Gerd von Runstedt, had dealt equally imperiously with the Russian frontier defences in its sector, south of the Pripet. This Army Group was a mixed one, consisting of a northern *masse de manoeuvre* of German infantry divisions, and a Panzergruppe, No 1, with to the south, an attached force of Rumanian divisions, and a Hungarian corps, all badly equipped with French weapons supplied during the years of the Little Entente. The satellite divisions' tasks were to affect a penetration on their front, east of the Carpathians, and then march in parallel with the German armies advancing into the Steppe of the Ukraine. Their object was Kiev, capital of the province and one of the most important industrial centres in Russia.

The initial penetration of the Army Group's allotted sector was followed, early in July, by one of the few recognisable large-scale counter-attacks mounted by the *Stavka* during the opening weeks of disaster. The Russian

Above left: Behind a fence on the border a motor-cycle unit awaits the order to advance. *Left:* German infantry catch sight of Brest, their objective

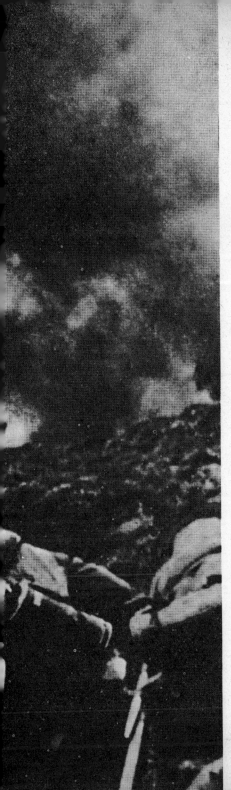

An assault section moves off behind
the barrage

Fifth Army, which had taken refuge
in the Pripet, and the Sixth Army,
operating out of the broad steppe,
attempted, rightly in terms of tactical
good sense, to pinch the head of the
German armed spearhead, represented
by Panzergruppe 1 advancing on Kiev,
by concentric attacks. In practice,
however, the unblooded Russian formations proved unable to shake the
battle-canny Germans, who quickly
formed defensive flanks, and then
mustered force enough to drive off
their attackers. The Russian effort
saved two of their Armies – Twelfth
and Twenty-sixth – from encirclement, but did not achieve its object.
On the contrary, it scarcely stayed
the advance of the Army Group, whose
disengaged panzers, racing ahead
again, had reached to within ten
miles of Kiev by 11th July.

The results of the fighting on the
fronts of the three Army Groups were
spectacular. It had carried Army
Groups North and South to within a
day's tank drive of each of their major
objectives, only a month after the
opening of the battle and, on Army
Group Centre's sector, had led to
hauls of prisoners and the infliction
of losses on a scale never contemplated before in war. It had, besides,
set new records for speed of advance:
Army Group Centre's spearheads were
on 15th July almost 500 miles
to the east of the point they had
started from on 22nd June. These
results not unnaturally led both OKH
and OKW, in the person of Hitler, to
believe that the 'Battle of Russia'
had been as good as finished within
the first four weeks and that all that
remained was to prevent the flight of
any more of the Red Army's broken
formations eastward. In deciding quite
how that was to be done, however, and
in assigning other tasks to the victor-
ious formations of the *Ostheer*, its
commanders were about to take
serious issue with each other.

71

Hitler and his generals disagree

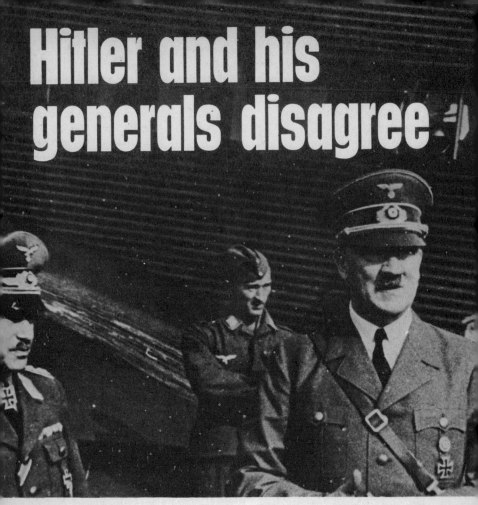

Hitler's confidence in his powers of military judgement had developed only slowly. Although he had been proved right, and his generals wrong, in believing that the German army's invasion of the Rhineland in 1936 and of Austria in 1938 would go unopposed, and although it was he again who was more accurate than they in forecasting the course and duration of the blitzkrieg against Poland in 1939, he was as yet unsure enough of his touch in great strategic matters to let the High Command of the Army prevaricate for long months during the winter of 1939–40 over plans for the invasion of the west. The High Command's reservations did not concern merely the nature or timing of the attack, but extended to questioning its necessity and even, in the case of von Leeb, its morality. Both Brauchitsch, the Commander-in-Chief, and Halder, the Chief of Staff (of OKH) tried to persuade Hitler, not once but several times, that an invasion of France by Germany, constituting as it would an assault on a stronger by a weaker power, was bound to culminate in disaster. Even after Hitler's peremptory and contemptuous dismissal of such fears, the generals had sought to delay the onset of the operation by proposing palpably half-hearted plans and advancing technical objections to the more promising proposals of others

(including Hitler himself).

In the event, the completeness of Germany's victory in the west went very far to establish Hitler, both in his own eyes and, at least for the time being, in those of his generals, as a strategist of the first quality. It would indeed have been unseemly for men who were ready enough to accept field marshal's batons from him (twelve were offered and none refused) to think otherwise. At the back of the German professional military mind, however, hovered a doubt about Hitler's talents at the level known as 'operativ': the level at which great strategic decisions are actually carried through, in the teeth of the enemy's efforts to thwart them – in short, the most difficult level of all. 'Operativ' skill, German military wisdom held, could be acquired only by long years of training and experience, both in peace and war, since its exercise demanded the most intimate acquaintance with the workings of all the subordinate formations of an army. That intimate acquaintance Hitler lacked, or appeared to do. Hence their mental reservations about the all-round quality of his military judgement, reservations to which support was lent by the evidence of his uncertainty of touch during the course of the operations in the west. The most important piece of that evidence concerned, of course, the decision to halt the armoured formations short of the Dunkirk perimeter on 26th May 1940, at a moment when the destruction of the B.E.F. lay within the Wehrmacht's grasp. As we now know, Hitler was prompted towards this decision by the advice of Runstedt, possessor of one of the most respected – and most orthodox – minds in the German Army. That consideration was, however, generally overlooked by a military caste which chose to think of Hitler as a man gifted with dazzling strategic insight but unsuited for the day-to-day management of forces in the field.

It would be strange indeed if they had held any other opinion, whatever the evidence. For not only was it undesirable for a Head of State to attempt to conduct military operations on any large scale by remote control (though Hitler was, of course, to do so for months and even years towards the end of the war). It was also quite contrary to the caste interest of the German *Generalität* to admit that such a thing was possible, for if they were once to abdicate their powers and responsibilities as battle-field commanders, to concede that a man at a map-table might better gauge the morale of their own men, better measure the strength and weaknesses of the enemy, better sense the temper

of the fighting and the approach of decisive opportunities, then their role as professional military executives was doomed to extinction, and they could look forward to a future in which they would act merely as messenger-boys of the Supreme Commander's will.

The very short duration of all the campaigns which the Wehrmacht had hitherto fought had precluded any persistent intervention by Hitler in their day-to-day management. An equally, perhaps more important factor had been the extraordinarily trouble-free way in which the great strategic plans had translated into action and achieved their designed results. For the first month of Barbarossa it seemed as if the pattern might repeat itself: the Führer's grand strategic vision unrolling majestically under the expert manipulation of the professional soldiers, on whom its creator kept no more than a benevolent and encouraging eye.

By the middle of July it was becoming apparent that this very satisfactory division of labour was about to break down. Given Hitler's character and the sheer scale of the Russian campaign, it could not have been otherwise. The numbers involved and the distances to be covered were so much greater than any the German army had yet faced, the objectives to be reached so much more widely dispersed, the aim to be attained so much more grandiose, that no planner, however percipient, and no plan, however comprehensive, could have provided for every contingency. On the contrary, 'operativ' skills of the highest order would be – were already proving to be – necessary if victory were to be wrested from the enemy within the time limits Hitler had set. Hence his incipient tinkering with the operational control of the forces now deployed across the steppe.

The vast distances of Russia blunted the impact of the infantry's advance

Hitler's medium of intervention in military affairs was the OKW (Oberkommando der Wehrmacht), in particular that section of it known as the Wehrmachtführungstab, led by Jodl. OKW's responsibilities had not originally been operational and were indeed still not supposed to extend to the control of operations in Russia (though they did in such 'OKW sectors' as North Africa and, by an odd quirk Finland). Day-to-day control of the armies in the field was exercised by OKH (Oberkommando des Heeres), the High Command of the Army. But it was at OKW, naturally, that Hitler held his twice daily situation conferences and there that the officers of OKH had to come to make their reports.

The two officers at the head of OKH, Brauchitsch and Halder, though devoted very strongly in principle to the operational autonomy of the Army were neither of them, unfortunately for the Army, of sufficiently strong character to defend that autonomy effectively. Halder, the Chief of Staff, possessed the intelligence to see the way things would go, were indeed going, if Hitler's steady erosion of OKH's powers continued, but lacked the capacity to oppose it. Brauchitsch, who might and should have stood firm, was the last officer likely to do so, since he had built his career on his appeasement of Hitler. Nominated to succeed Fritsch, after the latter had been dismissed on trumped-up charges of immorality in 1938, he had immediately acquiesced in the removal of several other senior officers unacceptable to his new masters, while accepting their help in expediting his own suit of divorce and re-marriage (to a rabid party member). Thereafter he had failed at almost every turn to stand up to Hitler; on the one occasion that he did, he chose his ground so badly and suffered such a torrent of vituperation by way of response that he may well have determined never to risk anything similar again.

Yet the necessity to stand up to

Hitler was now to be brought forward by the emergence of a genuine and profoundly important difference of opinion between him and his commanders in the field. In many ways this difference of opinion resembles that which was to overtake the Allied High Command in France, three years later, when, after the destruction of the *Westheer* in Normandy, Montgomery and Eisenhower were to disagree over how best their initial victory was to be exploited. Montgomery was to argue for a 'Narrow Front', an advance along a north-easterly axis, spearheaded by British troops and supported with all the transport and supply resources available to the Allied Forces, with the object of penetrating Germany's West Wall and capturing the Ruhr, her industrial heartland. Eisenhower, uneasy about the strength of the enemy forces which had escaped destruction or involvement in the Battle of Normandy, and fearful that the Allies' logistic resources could not be stretched the distance Montgomery wished to drag them, argued for and eventually insisted upon a 'Broad Front' advance by all the Allied armies, with the object of engaging the enemy on as wide a front as possible, of opening up several routes into Germany and of seizing bases from which to envelop rather than penetrate into the Ruhr.

The analogy is by no means a perfect one, since as we shall see Hitler pursued a more drastic solution to the Russian problem than Eisenhower would to his; but Montgomery and the German generals shared an identically radical attitude, while there were important similarities between the two logistic situations, which went equally unappreciated in 1941 and 1944. For the German Army found itself largely confined to the use of the roads to get supplies forward,

Brauchitsch, Commander of the Army, visiting a Luftwaffe unit on the Russian front

just as the Allies were to do in September 1944, though in the former's case not because of the destructive effects of its own air attack on the railway system but because of its need to reduce the Russian broad gauge (5 foot) railway track to standard Western European (4ft 8½in). Like Montgomery, however, the hard-riding panzer leaders would have no truck with complaints of the difficulties of sweating supplies forward over bad roads, broken down by the wear and tear of war, from distant bases to a constantly shifting front line.

Hitler first hinted at the trend of thinking which would bring him so sharply into conflict with his generals when on 8th July he made it clear that he was thinking, apparently because of the richness of the economic prize offered, of striking to capture the Ukraine rather than Moscow or Leningrad: a reversal of the strategic priorities laid down in the Barbarossa Order (Führer Direction No 21) which, after prescribing the destruction of the Red Army in Western Russia as the first aim, had stipulated that Leningrad and the Baltic coast be captured first and Moscow second unless very formidable circumstances made it possible to mount simultaneous operations directed against the two together. The Ukraine, in any case, was to come third.

The destruction of the Russian Army by envelopment was by mid-July already proving more of a meal than the jaws of the Panzer pincers could accommodate. Particularly troubling was the presence of a remnant of the Soviet covering force, represented by the Fifth Army, within the Pripet marshes. Post-mortems would later reveal that its striking power was small, but the menaces it levelled, against the flanks of both Army Group Centre, to its north, and Army Group South, were convincing enough to imply that these two major groupings were threatened along their rearward lines of communication. The

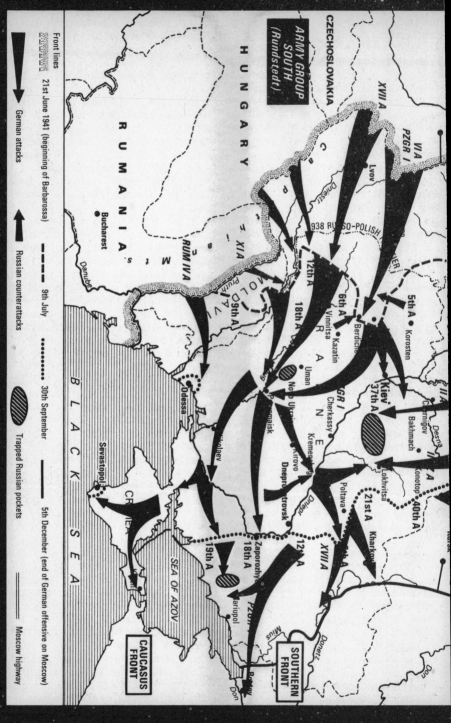

The Battle fronts 21st June – 5th December 1941

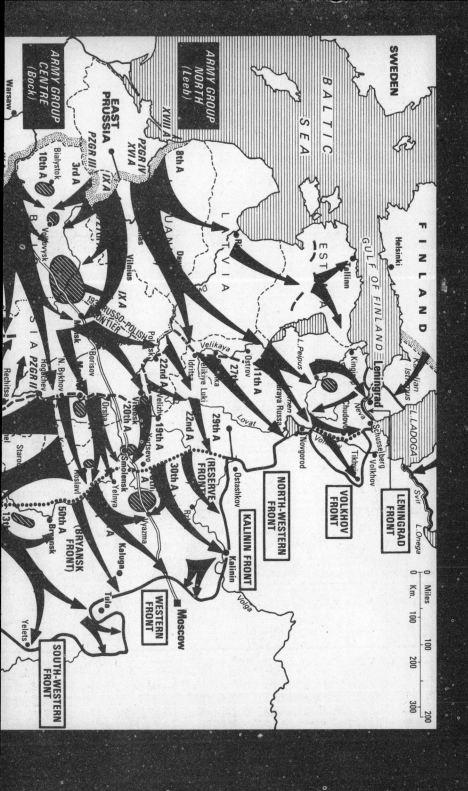

Soviet Fifth Army's own lines of communication with the interior remained, moreover, open.

On 19th July Hitler issued an important Führer Directive designed to clear up this situation. It re-emphasised that the primary aim of the operation was to destroy the Red Army west of the Dnieper-Dniestr line, in particular the Fifth Red Army in the Pripet and the Sixth and Twelfth Armies in the Ukraine, but laid down that these tasks were to be brought about by the diversion southward of a major part of the panzer strength of Army Group Centre. It was to concert attacks with the northern flank forces (the German Sixth Army and Kleist's Panzergruppe 1) of Army Group South. The rest of Army Group Centre's armour was to march to make contact with Army Group North and expedite its advance on Leningrad.

Here was interference by Hitler with operational control on a massive scale. Yet neither Brauchitsch nor Halder saw fit at this moment to take issue with him over it. Indeed, their view of the course of the fighting may well still have coincided generally with his. It was commanders at a lower level, notably panzer commanders, and in particular Guderian of Panzergruppe 2, who would react violently against this attempt of his to curtail the extent of their penetration of the mushy Russian defences to their front, and of their progress eastward.

They had as yet no means of conveying their feelings to Hitler who, growing more alarmed as the days passed at the intransigence of encircled Russian formations and perhaps already beginning to balance in his mind the comparative virtues of acquiring territory and destroying enemy forces, issued on 23rd July a supplement to Führer Directive 33 which rammed home its import. It

Guderian holds a Command
conference in the ruins of Roslavl,
August 1941

postponed the attack on Moscow until mopping-up operations around Smolensk had been concluded and would have entrusted the mission subsequently to infantry formations. Since the leading infantry units of Army Group Centre were still at least 220 miles from the capital, this passage of the Directive was clearly intended as an expression of aspiration rather than intent.

Russia's main concentration of force remained, moreover, on Army Group Centre's front, under Marshal Timoshenko, who was to launch against it a vigorous though inept counter-attack in the third week of July. In the fighting which followed both Guderian's and Hoth's panzer units suffered losses, none of which they could afford, since the wear and tear of the advance alone had now reduced their tank strength by 50 per cent.

Here was evidence to support Hitler's view, by no means one which OKH rejected, that 'the Russians will not be beaten by large-scale victories because they simply do not recognise that they have been beaten. They must therefore be smashed piecemeal by small tactical operations' (26th July). It was in terms of this thinking, and of the guide-lines laid down in the supplement to Directive No 33, that Brauchitsch now issued detailed orders to the operational headquarters.

As far as Army Group Centre's operations were concerned, he prescribed that it undertake first the destruction of the Soviet Fifth Army in the Pripet, using the *Panzergruppen*. Guderian, who had been called from his command post to hear these orders at a conference of Centre's Army commanders at its headquarters at Novi Borisow, was outraged at what he naturally regarded as this misuse of his tanks. Having also been promoted to the status of an army commander at this meeting, however (his panzergruppe being renamed accordingly *Armeegruppe Guderian*),

Guderian determined not to be bound by the instructions he had heard outlined there. In this determination he was to be much assisted by reason of the fact that his promotion freed him from the control of the commander of Fourth Army, Kluge, for whom he had a bitter dislike (which was returned). This left him directly answerable only to Bock, whose headquarters were appreciably further to the rear than Kluge's, and whose ideas on armoured warfare more nearly approximated to his own.

The technique on which Guderian settled as a means towards evading his unwelcome orders belongs to a venerable tradition in the history of military disobedience. He started a battle from which it proved impossible, at least by his representation of events, to disengage his force until it had won. The point at which he chose to organise this 'delaying action' was Roslavl, a small town seventy miles south east of Smolensk, lying between the Desna and the Dnieper, where the roads to Moscow, Leningrad and Kiev meet.

Guderian's declared motives, apart from gaining possession of so valuable a nodal point, was to break up what he declared to be a threatening concentration of Russian divisions in and around the town. The divisions, perhaps to the number of four or five, certainly existed but it seems unlikely that they were, as Guderian insisted in terming it, the spearhead of a major counter-attack. They seem to have been originally assembled, it must be admitted, with the object of breaking into the Smolensk pocket, either to extricate or to reinforce the units trapped therein.

In resorting to this evasion he appears to have enjoyed the approval, implicit or explicit, of Bock, his Army Group Commander, who cannot have cared for a redeployment of force which robbed him of the leading role of the Russian front, and also that of OKH, whose representative, appearing at Guderian's HQ on 31st July, let him know obliquely that the Army would not be hostile to some front-line resistance to Hitler's proclivity to dabble in operational affairs.

Whatever the attitude of Kluge or Bock or Halder, perhaps even of Hitler, it seems unlikely, however, that Guderian would have acquiesced in any decision that dispersed the panzer groups operating on what he regarded as the decisive axis, or even in a plan to divert them temporarily to other fronts. For Guderian, after all, had almost invented the panzer forces singlehanded, was certainly more closely identified with the principles of blitzkrieg tactics than any German general of his seniority and had unbounded confidence in their efficacy. To the panzer general, anxiety about the security of one's flanks or attempts to achieve secondary objectives *en passant* were equally anathema. Speed along the principal thrust line was what counted, for it was that which left the enemy breathless, spread disorganisation in his ranks, heightened his soldiers' bewilderment, cut his lines of approach to the threatened front, destroyed the infrastructure of his supply and transport system. On every ground, Guderian was predictably opposed to the closing down of the drive on Moscow, now only 220 miles from the forward patrol positions of his panzer troops. They had already come 440 miles in six weeks. Would it take longer to capture Moscow?

On the very evening of Guderian's Roslavl offensive, however, appeared a new Führer directive, No 34, which suggested that Hitler had had second thoughts. It laid down that the panzer groups of Army Group Centre were not to be lent out to its poorer neighbours. The central paragraph read: 'The development of the situation in the last few days, the appearance of stronger enemy forces on the front and to the flanks of Army Group Centre, the supply position and the need to give Panzergruppen 2 and 3 about ten days to rehabilitate their units makes it necessary to postpone for the moment further tasks and objectives.' Army Groups North and South were to make do with the forces presently under command and press forward.

Hitler's reasoning, if it was different from that outlined in the directive, has not been made clear. It may have been, however, that he accepted the inevitability of some delay at this moment (the German logistic system was very much in disarray and certainly could not have supplied the panzers in a 200 mile advance) and decided to profit from it by visiting the operational headquarters and attempting to form a personal impression of their circumstances and opinions. On 4th August he visited Army Group Centre at Novi Borosow. It was a visit fraught, though he did not know it, with risk, for Bock's entourage included several of that group of young aristocratic officers who were planning (in a rather dilettante fashion) to remove Hitler from power. Since they still shrank from violence against him, and were not unnaturally prevented by his SS guards from getting him to themselves, their efforts on this occasion misfired. It was an omen, nevertheless, of what they were to attempt with increasing purposefulness over the next three years.

Hitler, for his part, made a point of interviewing each of the Army commanders at Novi Borosow separately, lest their chorused objections to his strategy outweigh his defence of it. It was a sensible precaution, for when he asked Bock, Guderian and Hoth (commanding Panzergruppe 3) how long each would need to prepare his advance on Moscow, Bock declared himself ready to start at once, but Guderian requested a fortnight's and Hoth three weeks' warning. Re-assembled, they were unable to concert opposition to his plans and were even unable to wring from him a promise of satisfactory quantities of tank or tank part replacements for those destroyed or worn out in the advance – and this despite Hitler's extraordinary admission to Guderian that 'If I had known that the figures for Russian tank strength which you gave in your book (*Achtung! Panzer!* 1937) were in fact the true ones, I would not – I believe – ever have started this war'.

Hoth, whose Panzergruppe 3 had achieved as much as, if not more than, Guderian's, reacted to Hitler's deprecation of the Moscow thrust by obediently preparing his Panzergruppe for transfer to Army Group North's front. Neither Guderian nor Bock, nor indeed OKH, which had now plumped firmly for the Moscow option, showed anything like the same pliancy. Guderian, in fact, during what has been described as a 'nineteen-day interregnum' following Hitler's visit to Army Group Centre's HQ, did little that was positive; his object seems to have been to conserve as much force as he could on the Moscow front near Roslav, while edging reluctantly rightwards towards Army Group South as a gesture of compliance with Hitler's orders.

The Russian High Command seem to have shared Guderian's view, for they maintained their greatest strength on Army Group Centre's front and sent Timoshenko, who commanded there, the most plentiful reserves. Reserves at this time, however, rarely meant more than collections of the most hastily trained men, stiffened with cadres from training units in the interior or from divisions already destroyed in the fighting. It was reserves of this sort which also went to reinforce South-West Front, commanded by Budenny, who now began to assail the Stavka with requests to evacuate Fifth Army from its lodgement in the Pripet and add it to his disposable force. The Stavka rightly pointed out to him that if the German attack was presently hanging fire, that was due in part at least to the unwelcome presence of Fifth Army on the inner flanks of both Army Groups Centre and South. It accordingly refused Budenny permission to withdraw it, though it did order the creation of a new large formation, the Bryansk Front, which was to step forward into the gap opening up between Budenny and Timoshenko's commands.

As it happened, the Stavka was making the wrong decision for the right reasons. Any reading of the Germans' intentions, in terms of the blitzkrieg methods which seemed to have become their tactical and strategic orthodoxy, would point to Moscow as the focus of their effort in the secondary stage of the campaign. But what the Stavka could not know was that Hitler had come to doubt the validity of blitzkrieg methods in the vastness of Russia. Apart from his view that the Russians would not be beaten by large-scale victories, and that they would have to be smashed piecemeal by small tactical operations, he was also attracted by the economic prizes of the Baltic and Ukraine regions, whose loss to the Russians would so weaken their war-productive capacity, he argued, that battles for their possession would prove just as decisive as a new battle of encirclement to their most heavily defended sectors.

Thus although OKH and OKW, temporarily in accord after a meeting between Halder and Jodl on 7th August, were able to persuade Hitler into issuing a modification of Führer Directive 34 on 12th August, which laid the ground for a resumption of the advance towards Moscow, perhaps at the end of the month, some local setbacks suffered by Army Group North to the west of Leningrad three days later re-awoke his fears of failing to secure worthwhile material prizes, and provoked him into issuing another counter-order which would have detached individual panzer divisions from Army Group Centre to the northern front.

Bock called this order an 'impossible demand', since the armoured divisions earmarked were either refitting or in contact with the Russians, and appealed for support to Halder who, on finding Brauchitsch unwilling to act, convened the younger officers of operations section and had them compose an appreciation paper. Its conclusions were that an attack towards Moscow still offered the best chance of bringing the campaign to a swift and decisive end. Halder had it transmitted to Hitler and sent its principal author Colonel Heusinger to confer over its contents with Jodl. Their conversation, though known only in Heusinger's version, is revealing of the attitudes which prevailed at the time in the two rival (though temporarily allied) headquarters. Jodl declared that Hitler 'has an instinctive aversion to treading the same path as Napoleon. Moscow gives him a sinister feeling. He fears that there might be a life and death struggle with Bolshevism'. Heusinger apparently argued that that was precisely why the German army must seek to deliver battle there and when Jodl objected that the Führer's intuition was 'generally right' Heusinger raised the matter of Dunkirk again, saying that once more 'we are going to miss a decisive opportunity'.

Hitler's own reactions to the OKH operations officers' appreciation report were two: he issued, via Jodl, a new strategic instruction which directed the two outer Army Groups to proceed towards their objectives, Leningrad and Kiev – the Crimea – the Donetz basin, and Army Group Centre, without equivocation, to assist their progress; it stipulated, in particular, 'a concentric operation from the inner flanks of Army Groups South and Centre, against the Soviet Fifth Army'. He also prepared and sent to Brauchitsch, the Commander-in-Chief, a tactical study of the campaign which took the army in general (and Brauchitsch personally) to task;

Kluge, Guderian's rival for honours

Hoth, Commander of Panzergruppe 3

he former for its inept handling of the mobile forces, the latter for lack of the necessary grip'. Halder urged Brauchitsch to resign, offering to do so himself if he would, but the dispirited field-marshal (framing a sentiment which explains perfectly why under his leadership the German Army had lost all but the shreds of its former proud independence) declined to do so on the grounds that his resignation would not be accepted and that offering it would therefore effect nothing.

The most persistent proponent of the Moscow offensive, Guderian, was yet not to be stilled even by so emphatic a rejection of his case. He continued to believe that his Panzers could reach the capital and that at their approach the Russians, rallying everything to defend this centre of their communications and government, would expose themselves *en masse* to the decisive thrust. Halder, who had brought word of Hitler's decision to Bock and his subordinates at Army Group Centre on 23rd August, was sufficiently moved by Guderian's fervent exposé of the argument to agree that he should accompany him on his return to Rastenburg and put it to Hitler in person. They set off at once.

Arriving in time to make the onward journey to Hitler's evening conference, they were met by Brauchitsch, who began, 'I forbid you to mention the question of Moscow to the Führer. The operation to the south (the Kiev attack) has been ordered. The problem now is simply how it is to be carried out. Discussion is pointless'. Guderian thereupon 'asked permission' to fly back to the front, but Brauchitsch insisted that he report the situation of his Panzergruppe to Hitler 'but without mentioning Moscow'. So Guderian did; but with such heavy hints about the 'major objective' facing his front that Hitler himself broached the subject. Guderian, prompted to speak, outlined the 'central thrust' strategy with all the

precision and persuasiveness that informed his mind, and at some length. Hitler heard him out and then, in a riposte which included the words, not heard before by Guderian, that 'my generals know nothing about the economic aspects of war' explained the necessity he saw to secure the southern industrial region, from Kiev to Kharkov, and to neutralise the Crimea, from which he feared that Russia would mount air attacks against the Rumanian oil-fields.

Seeing that Hitler's entourage did not merely refrain from venturing a word in his support but actively endorsed, by gesture and murmurs of assent, every sentence that fell from Hitler's lips, Guderian forbore to press his argument. It was, after all, a strange enough situation to which he found himself, voicing, as a subordinate commander, views which his superiors held but would not admit to holding. Neither Brauchitsch nor Halder had accompanied him to the conference (so much for Brauchitsch's attempt to censor his report), yet when Guderian conveyed to Halder, the following morning, the gist of what had passed, including his own decision to acquiesce absolutely in the Führer's now unalterable resolve to shift the axis of attack against Kiev, and his request, accepted by Hitler, that his Panzergruppe be committed intact, Halder underwent what Guderian described as 'a complete nervous collapse'.

Pursued by his recriminations, indeed overtaken by them, for Halder was to telephone his very damaging version of these events to Army Group Centre Headquarters while Guderian was in flight, the latter arrived back at his Panzergruppe on 24th August. His purpose now was to conclude the Kiev operation swiftly and decisively enough to leave time for a re-opening of the 'decisive' attack on Moscow before the cold weather should descend. The German army would have only another two-and-a-half months.

The battle in the South

Army Group South, which was now to take on the principal role in Hitler's attempt to destroy the Red Army, had fought heretofore a less than glittering campaign. Its failure to achieve a quick and deep penetration was due in part to a lack of armour, for it controlled only one Panzergruppe (No 1, commanded by Kleist), and was encumbered with a collection of satellite divisions of several nationalities and miscellaneous equipment, the bulk obsolete. In ascending order of importance these foreign formations were: a Slovakian motorised division, a Hungarian motorised corps (of three brigades), an Italian expeditionary corps (of three divisions), the Rumanian Fourth Army, thirteen divisions strong, and another Rumanian Corps, of cavalry and mountain troops, under German command.

But its failure to penetrate had also been due to the great width of its front, nearly 600 miles from north to south. The front, moreover, was by no means badly defended, with four Russian Armies in covering positions, supported by four mechanised corps, with two more in reserve. Most important of all was the multiplicity of objectives which the Barbarossa directive allotted Runstedt. His northern wing, containing the bulk of the German units, was to force the frontier and split its axis of advance, Sixth

Army and Kliest's Panzergruppe 1 driving east to the Dnieper below Kiev, while Seventeenth Army headed south-east to reach the Dnieper below Vinnitsa. The two pincers claws were then to meet beyond the river and close fast on the Russians trapped between them. Meanwhile the southern wing, consisting of the Eleventh Army, and the satellite formations, after having protected the northern wing's flank against any Russian attempt at an enveloping manoeuvre, was to head due east, break Russian resistance in the Southern Ukraine, secure the Black Sea coast and form a front along the river Dnieper.

These were very ambitious plans, all the more so because the northern wing's axis of advance, initially at least, was very constricted, running as it did between the Pripet marshes to the north and the Carpathians to the south. Had the Russian Commander of the Kiev Military District, General Kirponos, got his covering plan right, he might well have given Runstedt a severe hammering in his passage along this cramped approach route, perhaps even stopped him in his tracks. But, as was happening elsewhere, he allowed his covering forces to be drawn piecemeal into the battle from the first day, instead of husbanding them for a counterstroke, and thus was to see them all destroyed.

His first notion was a good one, suggesting that he had studied the course of the German blitzkrieg against France and spotted how best to counter such tactics – which is, of course, by cutting into the flank of the armoured columns as it dashes past, if possible with an an equal or greater weight of armour. He had accordingly summoned to join his 22nd Mechanised Corps at Rovno the other three which were echeloned back in reserve. But before they could concentrate, he was forced to commit the 22nd to battle, in which it was consumed; its inexperienced tank crews and obsolescent vehicles were no match for Kleist's veterans in their Mark IVs. Moreover, when attacked, the Germans usually played the game, soon to become all too familiar to the British armour in the western desert, of falling back to entice the enemy onto an impenetrable line of 88mm guns. In this way another of Kirponos' mechanised corps, the 15th, attacking from its concentration area in the south, was also swiftly destroyed. And when the three divisions called forward from reserve arrived in the battle zone on 25-26th June they too were badly hammered, forced

to yield ground and to abandon men and equipment in profusion. Several of these losses were due to inept leadership. 'Corps Commissar Vashugin, ordered by Kirponos to mount a counter-attack with one-and-a-half tank divisions taken from Vlasov's IV Corps, took the tanks into a swamp, where they had to be abandoned. Vashugin committed suicide'. The Stavka, apparently concerned at the rate Kirponos was using up his armour, ordered him on 30th June to fall back to the 1939 frontier, which was fortified, and 'organise a stubborn defence with emphasis on anti-tank artillery weapons'.

This was not to be, however, the last attempt the South-West Front would make at amputating the tip of Kleist's panzer thrust. In the second week of July, the Fifth Army, which had been forced to withdraw from its covering position on the frontier into the Southern Pripet marshes, emerged from that impenetrable region to attack Panzergruppe 1 near Zhitomir. At the same moment another Russian army, the Sixth, struck north towards Berdichev in an attempt to link hands. The Germans, in whom two years of war had developed considerable all-round tactical skills, were able, though at first outnumbered, to ride out this heavy and concerted attack. The T-34 tank, of which the Germans were eventually to form so respectful an opinion that at one time they considered copying and mass-producing it for their own panzer divisions, made one of its earliest appearances in this counter-attack. But faulty tactical handling, and the penetrative power of the 88mm flak gun, firing at zero elevation, nullified its effect on this occasion. Badly battered, the Sixth Army fell back south-eastward while the Fifth Army retired once more northward into Pripet marshes,

where its presence was gravely to deform the development of German strategy throughout the next six weeks – and this despite the fact that its striking power had now been quite blunted.

The consequences of Fifth Army's eccentric withdrawal were not yet fully perceived, certainly not by the staff of Army Group South, which had its eyes fixed on the Russian deployment to its front. Budenny, the flamboyant but obtuse Red cavalryman whom Stalin had appointed to lead the South-West Front on 10th July, with Nikita Kruschev as his political commissar, had opted to concentrate the bulk of his disposable forces, which grew daily in size as Stalin fed with reinforcements what he was now coming to view as the most vulnerable and vital sector of the battle-front, at two widely separated points: Kiev and Uman. Kiev, the capital of the Ukraine, and indeed the ancient capital of Russia, was by far the more tempting of these two nodal points at which to strike. Runstedt decided, however, that it should not be attacked. His reasons were various but consistent: the city lay off the main axis of the two Army Groups' advances, which ran generally south-eastward towards the Black Sea and the lower courses of the great south Russian rivers, the Bug, Dnieper and Donetz; a major diversion of force would be necessary to invest and capture it, since the city was large and numerously, if not well, defended; and this operation would involve some of the panzer divisions in the sort of close fighting for which they were unsuited, and at a moment when they should be deepening the German penetration. Accordingly he left orders that the two panzer divisions nearest, 13th and 14th under General Mackensen, should attack only if presented with the most favourable opportunities. Meanwhile he was probing for an opening further south. Though not

Officers of the Italian Expeditionary Corps are presented to Kleist, commander of Panzergruppe 1

T-34 tanks in a German battlefield scrapyard

a panzer general himself – being the most senior serving general officer of the German army, his tactical thinking had been formed long before the tank had come into its own – Runstedt nevertheless knew how to let his panzer commanders handle their formations, and when Kleist alerted him to an evident weakness in the Russian line covering the main north-south railway on Budenny's front, he gave him permission to exploit it. Kleist was quickly through and racing eastward to outflank the concentration areas around Uman from the north. Despite the menace that this thrust suspended above the Russian forces concentrated there, Stalin and Budenny continued to reinforce them, while preparing to launch another of those ill-fated counter-attacks which had cost the Red Army so dear throughout the preceeding month. The force earmarked was the Twenty-Sixth Army which, with a carelessness for which Russian staff-officers had become notorious during the First World War, allowed its operation order to fall into enemy hands. When its counter-attack began, on 20th July, the Germans easily broke it up, all the more so because of the particularly crude frontal fashion in which it was launched.

The trend of Kleist's operations was now becoming clear, even to the Russians. It was evident that he was headed for the Kiev-Dnepropetrovsk railway, the securing of which would isolate Uman from the rear. On 25th July Kleist's leading tanks entered Novo Ukraina and on 30th July were firmly established across the railway between that town and Kirovo, to the north. The only escape route still left open to the Russian Sixth, Twelfth and Eighteenth Armies following this coup lay southeastwards, along the lower course of the River Bug to the Black Sea at Nikolaev. It offered a chance which the

Russians seemed intent on refusing. By 3rd August, they had delayed too long. Schobert, the German commander on the right or 'satellite' wing of Army Group South, after seizing bridgeheads across the Bug, had managed to find a way round the flank of a determined Russian blocking force for two of his own divisions and had raced them along the river to Pervomaisk. It was there on 3rd August that they made contact with the leading elements of XIV Panzer Corps, sent southwards by Kleist specifically to meet them.

These Russian prisoners had probably only a few weeks training

The Uman region had now become a pocket, or cauldron *(Kessel)* as the German Army called it. The next task was to stitch its sides more tightly for, as it was always the case with cordons drawn by armour and motorised units alone, the Germans' blocking positions were as yet by no means proof against break-outs. Not until 8th August, when the infantry divisions of Eleventh and Seventeenth Armies at last got forward to the armour, after days spent marching on abominable roads under a boiling sun, could Runstedt reckon on having pulled off an encirclement to equal those achieved by Bock's armies on the central front. His tally of losses inflicted on the enemy amounted to

fifteen infantry and five armoured divisions destroyed and 103,000 prisoners taken.

This German success on the upper sector of the Army Group South's front now unlocked the lower, coastal, sector for the Rumanians. The most tempting focus for attack was provided by the naval base of Odessa, and the Stavka was consonantly determined to defend it to the last. It had ordered, and work had already begun on, the construction of a defensive perimeter three lines deep and, measured overall, 400 miles long, with emplacements for over a hundred battalions. The Rumanian IV Corps arrived outside the fortress in early August and completed the

investment of these formidable defences on 14th August. The city was now isolated by land. But the siege was to last sixty-four days and cause the Rumanians, who had already suffered heavy losses in the frontier battles, an almost unbearable toll of casualties.

The battle of Odessa, like many sieges, was to become eventually an affair on its own. In its earliest stages, however, it had a crucial effect upon the course of the fighting in general on Budenny's front, for the Stavka's decision to concentrate forces inside its lines was to mean that the defence of the Bug and Dnieper was to be severely hampered. This was all the more serious in that at the same moment a similar gap which had

Left: PzKw Mark II tanks wade a tributary of the Desna on Guderian's drive to the South. *Above:* Infantry cross the Desna in assault boats

opened north of Kiev towards the middle of July, as the Central and South-Western fronts were driven away from each other under German pressure, remained unfilled. Kiev, which now harboured the most important Russian concentration on the whole battlefront between the Baltic and the Black Sea, thus lay temptingly vulnerable to a double envelopment.

Stalin and the Stavka were by no means unaware of the danger which impended from the isolation of the Central from South-Western Front and on 16th August created a new Bryansk Front in order to close the gap between them. Its command was given to General Yeremenko, though he was given only two infantry armies, plus the promise of others which had already met the enemy, in order to carry out his functions.

Meanwhile, the Stavka gave its permission, which Budenny had been seeking for some days, for all his units west of the Dnieper to be withdrawn to the east bank of the river. Thirty-Seventh Army was to be left in Kiev, while Fifth Army, released at last from its vigil in the Pripet, and Fortieth Army, a scratch formation of battle-weary units, were ordered to form front along the line Kharkov-Konotop-Chernigov, as a further precaution against any attempt by the Germans to penetrate the gap between Central and South-Western commands.

Such a threat was in the process of organisation, Guderian having already re-deployed his Panzergruppe on a southern axis. He was now ready to lead it towards Kiev. But on the same day that Guderian had left Hitler's headquarters after his failure to persuade him of the case for pressing forward against Moscow, Yeremenko got word from Stalin of the importance

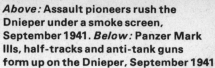
Above: Assault pioneers rush the Dnieper under a smoke screen, September 1941. *Below:* Panzer Mark IIIs, half-tracks and anti-tank guns form up on the Dnieper, September 1941

attached by the Stavka to the counter-thrust he was to launch. Stalin offered him attractive quotas of new equipment: several T-34 tank battalions and some of the new Katyusha rockets, a multiple-barrelled mortar firing light fin-stabilised projectiles with very large warheads. The dissolution of the Central Front on 25th August added another two armies to his order of battle, the Thirteenth and Twenty-First. Unfortunately, the dissolution of the Central Front led Yeremenko to believe that he was also responsible for the defence of the approach routes to Moscow – a word of warning on the ambiguity of German intentions from Shaposhnikov, the Chief of Staff, encouraged him in this belief – and he accordingly divided his force, allotting the best of it to what was to turn out to be a completely passive front.

Guderian noted impassively on 29th August that his XXIV Panzer Corps had come under attack from the south and west. He was referring to the opening of Yeremenko's counter-offensive. Supported though it was by the bulk of the tactical air force which still remained to the Red Army – about 500 aircraft – it never properly developed an impetus. Twenty-First Army, which spearheaded the attack, was rapidly outflanked, to left and right respectively by Kluge's Fourth Army and Guderian's Panzergruppe 2. Forced into a hasty retreat, it carried with it a number of its own supporting units and left gaping holes in the front through which the German motorised units at once began to infiltrate at speed and in strength.

While Guderian was breaching Kiev's northern defences, Kleist, whose Panzergruppe had just pulled off so successful an encirclement at Uman, was redeploying it to attack northwards in a convergent

Above: Kiev burns, September 1941.
Left: the ruins of Kiev, ancient capital of Russia

manoeuvre. While the business of transferring units went on, the reconnaissance units of the Panzergruppe were establishing a series of small bridgeheads across the Dnieper between Cherkassy and Kremenchug, a sector held by only one Russian infantry army, the Thirty-Eighth. Its front was far too long for it to defend and its equipment state in no way fitted it to fight the panzer battalions of Kleist. Its rear, moreover, was coming under threat of attack from units of Reichenau's Sixth Army which was pressing eastward, following its final reduction of the Uman pocket.

In the last week of August, therefore, all the signs spoke of an impending German encirclement of Kiev and hence of a catastrophic Russian defeat on the southern front. Yet Stalin's reaction to all suggestions that troops should be withdrawn from the threatened region before it was too late, or even that they should be allowed to withdraw to more defensible positions, was rejection. On the contrary, he sought troops with whom to swell the already bloated garrison of the Ukrainian capital, and was ready to strip the most sensitive sectors of the front in order to do so. As a result of his intervention, nearly one million men were to fall or come within a hair's breadth of falling into German hands.

Of the twin prongs of the panzer thrust, that formed by Guderian's Panzergruppe 2 had further to come and the harder battle to fight on the way. Indeed its fighting advance was an extraordinarily risky one, since it had progressively to expose its left flank to attack from the east. Its exposed flank was eventually to stretch for over 150 miles. Had the Russians been organised to launch co-ordinated attacks, they could well have destroyed him. But bitterly though such Russians as his soldiers met were prepared to fight, they were already showing all the signs of that disorganisation to which two months of combat had reduced them. Startling evidence of their disorientation was provided, on 26th August, by 3rd Panzer Division's success in capturing intact a 750-yard long bridge over the River Desna at

Novgorod Severski. Guderian, in his strangely deadpan record of the operation, describes the feat, carried out by a Lieutenant of the 6th Panzer Regiment, as 'surprising and most gratifying'. Equally striking is the footnote to his account of the events of 3rd September: that on that day, the commanders of 3rd and 17th Panzer Divisions, Model and Ritter von Thoma, of whom the first was later to become a field-marshal, the second to be captured as commander of the Afrika Korps, both suffered minor wounds in the course of duty. Leading from the front, which these 'new', young generals made a habit, was altogether more dangerous against an enemy who, unlike the French in 1940, did not surrender when by-passed.

Guderian's Panzergruppe was to fight this confused sort of battle for the next eighteen days, struggling to overcome for much of that time not only enemy opposition but the obstacles to progress created by heavy rainfall: swollen streams, flooded bridges and many miles of liquid mud on the surface of the bad and infrequent roads. Often his motorised formations moved scarcely faster than the infantry divisions of Second Army, which were pressing inward on South-West Front to his right.

While Guderian beat his way down from the north, Kleist in the south was manoeuvring to swing his Panzergruppe onto a convergent axis. His object was to bring his armour up against the northern reach of the great Dnieper bend and force crossings. Since the river between Cherkassy and Kremenchug was defended by only a single Russian Rifle Army (Russian Armies were smaller than German, and this one lacked any armour), the tactical difficulties of seizing bridgeheads against its opposition were unlikely to prove great. In fact it was not until 12th September that Kleist had finally secured an adequate pas-

Krushchev, then a military commissar

Yeromenko, Commander of the Bryansk Front

A scouting patrol is sent forward

sage but he had virtually destroyed the Russian Thirty-Eighth Army in so doing. On 16th September at Lokhvitsa, a hundred miles north of Kremenchug, his tanks and Guderian's made contact. Within the next few days, the infantry divisions of both Panzergruppen made their way forward to close the gaps in the armoured cordon. Behind them Seventeenth Army, moving north on Kleist's left, and Second Army, moving south on Guderian's right, increased the pressure on the Kiev pocket. Reichenau's Sixth Army, marching east from Uman, meanwhile worked to constrict the pocket along its western face while, from the air, the 2nd and 4th Air Armies of Kesselring and Löhr inflicted an unbearable toll of casualties on the packed masses of Russian troops.

By 26th September, the battle of Kiev had to all intents ended. On that date, the German official news service announced that the pocket had yielded up 665,000 Russian prisoners, 884 tanks and 3,718 guns. Five Russian Armies and fifty divisions had been destroyed. The Russians have subsequently disputed these figures, claiming that their losses totalled no more than 175,000. It is impossible to reconcile these figures; but although the German reckoning is breathtakingly large, contemporary reports would suggest that it is a more convincing estimate than the Russian.

More interesting than attempts to compute the casualties is to enquire why the Russian High Command should have allowed so many of its soldiers to remain in positions which were so clearly at risk for more than a fortnight before their fall. The subject is one which has provoked bitter and, since Krushchev's anti-Stalin speech in 1956, public debate in the Soviet Union. Krushchev, as Political Commissar of the South-West Front, is of course a prejudiced witness, all the more so because he is able to

contrast Stalin's allegedly inept refusal to withdraw the garrisons of Kiev with his own success in evacuating large quantities of industrial equipment from the threatened area. Nevertheless it is true that he supported Budenny in his protest at Stalin's orders to stand fast – the protest which led to Budenny's 'transfer' on 13th September to an honorific post with the Reserve Front. Budenny's removal did not however lead to any stilling of voiced opposition from the South-Western Front, which protested the orders laid upon it right up to the moment of its encirclement. Not until twenty-four hours after the circle had been closed did Stalin relent. Those who were able to take advantage of this relaxation of his strictures to stand fast were few. Many who did try to break out were killed as they passed through the German lines, including several generals, Kriponos, the Front Commander, among them.

The fate of those Russian soldiers who suffered capture instead of death outside Kiev was lamentable. Germany and Russia were not bound by the Geneva Convention on the treatment of their prisoners, but the normal conventions of warfare demand that a captured enemy shall be fed and sheltered. The German army, deliberately or by default, failed to observe those standards during the opening months of Barbarossa. Of the *four million* Russians taken prisoner between June 1941 and February 1942, over half a million were to die between November 1941 and January 1942 alone. Many had already succumbed to neglect or the effect of untreated wounds. Thereafter, no Russian lightly chose capture as an alternative to further resistance.

Conversely the German soldier, aware of the fear and hatred which the news of such treatment of prisoners had aroused among the Russians, would also often fight to the death rather than risk capture. The 'war without chivalry' for which Hitler

The port of Odessa after a German raid

Russian sailors armed as infantry
march up to the Odessa defences

had wished was thus not slow to materialise.

While the Kiev battle raged, other sectors of the Southern front were crumbling under German attack. A most important focus of fighting was Odessa, the Black Sea Port, which had been invested by the Rumanians on 5th August. There the Russian defenders; marines, soldiers and sailors of the hastily constituted Special Maritime Army of General Petrov, were to hold out until 16th October, and to inflict 100,000 casualties on their besiegers. After the fall of the city, it was to be incorporated into Rumania as capital of the new Rumanian province of Transniestria, a distinction which, since it permitted many Odessans to resume their agreeable pre-Revolutionary habits of life, proved remarkably popular in the city.

Of far greater military significance was the initiative undertaken by Runstedt's Eleventh Army, now commanded by a General von Manstein (of whom the Russians were to hear more), which between 21st and 29th September was able to force the estuary of the Dnieper and advance as far as the neck of the peninsular of the Crimea. This advance threatened to turn all the Russian defences of the Southern rivers – Donetz and Don – and of their great industrial centres. Whether Hitler would encourage Runstedt to make that attempt or whether he would listen to the arguments for renewing the attack in the centre or the north had now become the principal strategic issue. Kharkov? Moscow? Leningrad? Decisions over operations against the latter, most tangible of all the objectives allotted a German commander, had proved as difficult as any Hitler had had to take during the campaign thus far and had not yet led to a satisfactory solution of the 'Leningrad problem'. It was to continue to distort Hitler's strategic judgement.

The investment of Leningrad

Leningrad is unmistakeably a capital city: the great width of its streets, the splendour and scale of its buildings, the dramatic quality of its townscape, proclaim that it was planned and built as a seat of government. And so indeed it was, by the Great Tsar, Peter I, at the beginning of the eighteenth century, on a site reclaimed from the marshes of the river Neva and the coastal swamps of the Gulf of Finland. Leningrad is thus also a port, the most important in Russia, and the centre of her naval power in Western waters. Western is the keynote: built by Peter as his 'window' on the Europe of Louis XIV, Leningrad – Petrograd, St Petersburg, as it had been called in turn – had always been and looked, as it still remained, the most Western of all Russian cities; Western enough, in 1917, to have provided the cast for a series of political crises of a range and intensity unseen in Europe since the fall of the *Ancien Régime* – beginning

with discontent in the constitutional assembly and ending in full-blown Communist revolution.

The transfer in 1918 of the seat of government from Leningrad – as Petrograd was renamed after the leader's death – to Moscow robbed the city of its paramount status; but though it wounded it did not diminish the Leningraders' pride in their city – or indeed, in themselves, whom they thought formed the most sophisticated and outward looking society in Soviet Russia. Nor did it mean that the Soviet government thereafter valued Leningrad any less highly than the Tsars had Petersburg or cared less for its security or paid less heed to its mood. The political temper of the Leningrad party organisation – which tended, in Moscow's view, to unreliability – was a constant concern of Stalin and the defence of the city was to become, in the late 1930s, an obsession with him. It was because of his

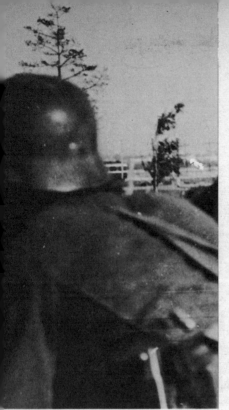

German machine gunners look across the River Neva to Leningrad, September 1941

vasion of Russia, launched his own troops across the border in June 1941. The Finnish army was not large but it knew how to defeat the Russians, whose reserves, in any case, were occupied on more important fronts; and it was assisted by important contingents of German troops on its northern flank, forming the *Norwegen Armee* under General Dietl and consisting of the III, XXVI and Mountain Corps, six divisions in all. These German troops had landed on and after 8th June, Finnish general mobilisation following on 16th June, their declaration of war on 25th June.

The Germans counted on a great deal of help from the Finns who, they believed, were as anxious to deal Soviet Russian a death-blow as they were themselves. In this, as events would show, they were mistaken. The Finns were indeed eager for battle, and were delighted to be fighting at the Germans' side, but their aims were purely national and quite limited. Mannerheim, the Finnish leader, was resolved that as soon as these aims had been achieved the Finnish Army would stand fast.

The aims of the Germans themselves on this northern front had been laid down in the Barbarossa directive. They were to destroy the enemy forces operating in the Baltic area and to occupy Leningrad and Kronstadt, the island naval base at the mouth of the Neva. These were considerable tasks, since the distance from the eastern border of East Prussia to Leningrad was 500 miles, more if the coast is followed, as this plan demanded that it had to be, while the force allotted to Army Group North was the weakest of all three: twenty infantry divisions, shared between the Sixteenth and Eighteenth Armies, and three armoured and three motorised divisions belonging to General Hoepner's

desire to deepen the cordon of national territory between the city and the outside world that he had been led to make unacceptable territorial demands of the Finns in 1939, to wage war against them and eventually, after the humiliating defeats of that winter, to annex from them large areas of the Karelian isthmus and of the frontier region north of Lake Ladoga. (This, one of the largest lakes in Europe, lies immediately inland of Leningrad and almost isolates it from the interior).

These annexations of Stalin's, for which there were excellent justifications of a purely military sort, took no account of the probability that Finland would seek to recover what had been taken from her, and would choose to do so when Russia was least able to prevent her. Stalin, in short, had, for little concrete advantage, unnecessarily made an enemy who, true to expectations and simultaneous with Germany's in-

113

Marshal Mannerheim, the Finnish
leader

Küchler, Commander of
Eighteenth Army

Manstein, a master practitioner of
war on the steppe

A German anti-tank gun and crew block a road at Kovno

Riga's welcome for the Germans expressed a genuine sense of liberation

Panzergruppe 4. Perhaps the most remarkable thing about the Army Group was that both its commander, Ritter von Leeb, and the GOC of one of its armies, Küchler of the Eighteenth, had been dismissed by Hitler in the aftermath of the Blomberg-Fritsch crisis. They had restored their good standing during the campaign in the west.

The tactical planning of Army Group North's operation was comparatively complicated, for the conformation of this sector of Russian territory into which it had to attack made it unlikely that it would be able to bring off anything in the way of a major encirclement, while two rivers, the Niemen and the Dvina, provided the Russians with defensible water obstacles running athwart the line of advance. That line of advance, moreover, was seriously constricted on the immediate approaches to Leningrad by Lakes Peipus and Ilmen, between whose waters Army Group North would have to direct its final thrust. Opposing its onset was a considerable Russian force: the Eighth, Eleventh, and Twenty Seventh Armies on the frontier which, with between whose waters Army Group supports and reserves, totalled twenty-eight infantry divisions and three mechanised Corps, with a strength of a thousand tanks. The North-Western Front, to which these units were subordinated as soon as war began, was commanded by Colonel-General Kuznetsov (who was later to be replaced by Voroshilov), a competent if not brilliant soldier.

Leeb's solution to his problem of movement was to place his armoured formations in the centre of his front, with the infantry armies on the flanks. His reasoning was that since he could not hope to organise large-scale pincer movements, he would attempt to destroy the Russian front

A Waffen SS heavy machine gun team in a Lithuanian village

by sharp, deep and repeated armoured thrusts, along a single line of penetration. The disruption this caused would, he hoped, leave those Russians by-passed by his armour so shattered that the German infantry, following up as close behind the panzers as possible, would be able both to protect their own flanks, net prisoners in quantity and secure geographical objectives of importance. Leeb intended to keep the Panzergruppe under his personal command, which meant that at times he would be communicating directly with Hoepner's Corps Commanders. One of these, Erich von Manstein, was a soldier with the makings of a world reputation.

The Panzergruppe's first objectives beyond the East Prussian border were the bridges across the Dvina, the widest river of Russia's Baltic Coastland. (Hitler's pre-war annexation of the Free City of Memel provided, very conveniently, the necessary crossings of the Niemen, which formerly de-limited East Prussia's eastern boundary). These bridges lay 150 miles distant from Hoepner's start line, across terrain which, though the Russians had had little chance to fortify it since their own annexation of Lithuania and Latvia in 1940, formed nevertheless a strongly defended zone, all the more so because of the size of the Russian garrison. And indeed the first news that Hoepner had of the prospects of his operation on 22nd June was of a strong Russian armoured column marching to meet the spearheads of his LVI Panzer Corps at the road junction of Kedaynyay, just across the frontier. For once it was the speed of the enemy rather than the Germans which spared them a head-on collision: the Russian column had passed through and on from Kedaynyay by the time LVI Corps' tanks reached it. Leaving XLI Panzer Corps to deal with the situation there, Manstein pressed his divi-

Above: A light flak gun outside Grodno, June 1941. *Left:* The pace of movement along Russian roads was slow

which it embarked the day following, 2nd July. Its new objectives lay on the 'little land bridge' between the two lakes, Peipus and Ilmen, along a line which also marked the old Latvian-Russian frontier and was likely to be covered by the fortification of the 'Stalin line'. The three points on the line which it was particularly vital to seize were, from north to south, Pskov, Ostrov and Opochka, all on the River Velikaya, which flows into Lake Peipus.

The first of these places to be reached was Ostrov, on 4th July. It was taken unopposed, for the Russians appear to have expected the Germans to align their advance further to the north and had massed their armour around Pskov. When they swung it southward to engage XLI Corps on 5th July, this force was almost completely destroyed, 140 of its tanks remaining as punctured or burnt-out carcasses on the battlefield north of Ostrov. Pskov fell at once into XLI Corps' hands; LVI Corps had already moved on Opochka.

Panzergruppe 4 had now made over half the distance on its road to Leningrad. At this point, however, the pace of its advance was too slow, in part because of difficulties in maintaining the flow of supplies to the forward units, but also for two more important reasons: the encounter by the panzer divisions of a wide sector of 'untankable' terrain athwart their axis of advance, and the unsettling effect of the High Command crisis of July on the tactical direction of Army Group North.

The terrain in question was a marshy belt along the far bank of the river Velikaya, on the old Latvian-Russian border. It was least passable east of Opochka, from which crossing-place Manstein's LVI Panzer Corps was supposed to lead a thrust towards Novgorod, on the river Luga, Leningrad's outermost defence line. Several attempts to press forward through the swamps quickly proved the infeasability of the plan and LVI was accor-

sions forward towards the Dvina. On the morning of 26th June the leading tanks of 7th Panzer Division swept into Daugavpils and seized its two bridges. Their advance had been an astonishing achievement, even by panzer standards, for they had made good at least thirty-five miles a day for four days. Hoepner now hurried forward XLI Corps which, since left by LVI Corps, had enveloped and destroyed completely the Russian armoured force which had so alarmed Hoepner on 22nd June. He now ordered it to secure bridgeheads downstream of LVI's at Daugavpils. By 1st July it had done so, and eighteen miles of the far bank of the Dvina had consequently been brought under German control.

By makeshift means, sufficient fuel and munitions were brought forward to the Panzergruppe to provision it for the second stage of the advance, on

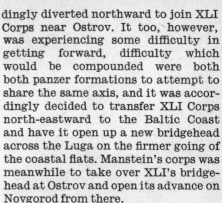

dingly diverted northward to join XLI Corps near Ostrov. It too, however, was experiencing some difficulty in getting forward, difficulty which would be compounded were both both panzer formations to attempt to share the same axis, and it was accordingly decided to transfer XLI Corps north-eastward to the Baltic Coast and have it open up a new bridgehead across the Luga on the firmer going of the coastal flats. Manstein's corps was meanwhile to take over XLI's bridgehead at Ostrov and open its advance on Novgorod from there.

The plan was not one which recommended itself to Manstein, who believed that, *coute qui coute*, the Panzergruppe should be kept united and used to deliver a single, solid punch – orthodox blitzkrieg thinking. But neither Hoepner nor Leeb, however much they might sympathise with his reasoning, had the freedom to give the necessary orders. From the middle of July onwards Leeb was under instructions to help forward the left wing of Army Group Centre, a task which entailed the diversion of infantry from Sixteenth Army on his own right flank towards Army Group Centre's left, a diversion which, in turn, left Manstein unprotected and so made it impossible for Leeb to sanction any specially deep or fast penetration towards Leningrad by his tanks. Indeed Leeb had to stipulate in late July that any continued advance by Manstein's LVI Corps must be in the company of a strong infantry escort from which it was to be allowed to cut loose only after the two had managed to destroy the most dangerous of the Soviet concentrations threatening the tanks' advance in the vicinity of Lake Ilmen.

This advance proved in practice to be a bloody and exhausting one, particularly for the infantry, and by the beginning of August Leeb had decided to abandon the notion, which he had originally entertained and which still

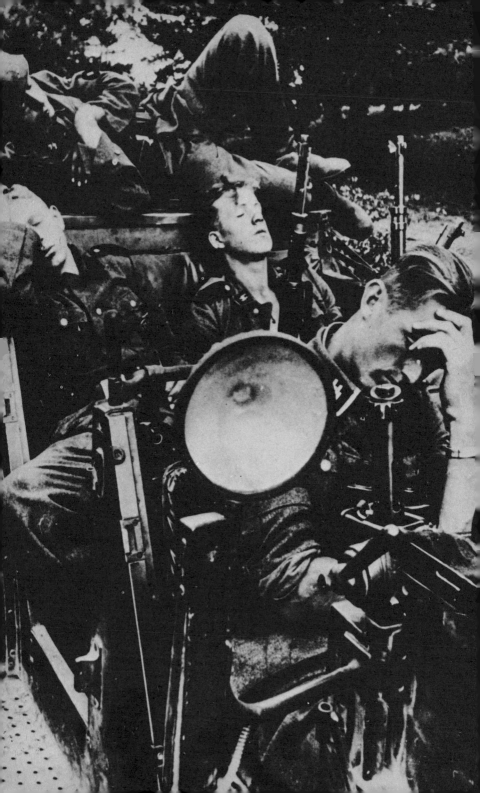

Left: Waffen SS troops resting on the road to Leningrad. *Above:* Summer rain at Kingissep, August 1941

obsessed the gauchos of the Panzer divisions, of a lightning descent on Leningrad itself. Instead he took up the project of a double envelopment of the city by the two panzer corps, supported on either flank by the infantry Armies, Eighteenth and Sixteenth, all acting in concert with the Finns, who were to advance southwards along the Karelian Isthmus and south-eastward round the inner shore of Lake Ladoga.

For the Germans, their initial role in this plan was to break across the last major obstacle on the road to Leningrad, the Luga river, which flows northwestward from Lake Ilmen to the Gulf of Finland. They already controlled bridgeheads on the far shore, only sixty miles from Leningrad. The task now was to concentrate major forces inside these bridgeheads and smash the Russian forces manning the river line. These, which belonged to the North-Western Front, were divided between three sectors: the Kingisepp, where three infantry divisions were posted, the Luga, defended by another three and the Eastern, near Lake Ilmen, held by a scratch division and a mountain brigade. Besides these, there were also stragglers and broken units, though what fighting strength they added to the defence was dubious.

Its fighting strength by any reckoning was low and though, when the German attack came in on 8th August, the Russian soldiers fought as bravely as they always did in fixed positions, their lack of artillery and armour put them at an irremediable disadvantage. By 11th August, the Kingisepp sector had been almost breached and the commander of the river line, Popkov, was contemplating a withdrawal, though where he would

Above: Novgorod burning under German bombardment. *Above right:* The Germans reached the suburbs of Leningrad at the end of August

retire to and under cover of what rearguard even he could not explain. Manstein's LVI Corps, disengaged by Leeb from the right flank, was moving towards the Kingisepp breach; once arrived, it would leave Popkov no option about staying or going. At almost that moment, however, temporary deliverance was granted the expiring Russian defence. Their Thirty-Eighth Army, part of the Finnish frontier garrison which had moved southward undirected round the eastern shore of Lake Ilmen, suddenly appeared on the unprotected flank of Leeb's Sixteenth Army and gave it and Leeb a serious fright. Although the attacking force was composed mainly of cavalry, Leeb ordered Manstein back post haste from his mission to Kingisepp, a journey of over a hundred miles which LVI Corps had only just completed. Thirty-Eighth Army was quickly repelled and the German advance at once regained its impetus. Novgorod fell on 16th August and Chadovo on 20th August. But despite the arrival of a fresh Panzer Corps (XXXIX) from Panzergruppe 3 – part of the redistribution of armour ordered by Hitler after the Rastenberg conference with

Guderian – Manstein's LVI Corps found it difficult to make as much headway as XLI Corps which, on 21st August, reached Krasnogvardeisk, only thirty miles from Leningrad. Instead of pressing home this thrust, Leeb decided that the Corps should turn southward and effect a junction with Manstein near Novgorod, thus destroying the resistance which impeded LVI Corps' advance and encircling what looked like the sizeable Russian forces still in position on the Luga or about to retreat from it. This junction was completed on 31st August, and the resulting encirclement yielded a bag of 20,000 prisoners.

The battle to encircle Leningrad was now entering its final stage. 'Encircle' was still the operative principle, for Hitler had not ordered the city to be captured. But to do even as much as that effectively depended on the co-operation of the Finns, who were showing themselves reluctant to cross the 1939 frontiers, all of which they had now recovered. On 22nd August, OKW

had asked Mannerheim to extend his advance down the Karelian isthmus so as to outflank Leningrad from the north and join hands with the Germans to the east of the city. Mannerheim had delayed answering until 27th August when he told OKW that he was prepared to meet the Germans on the Svir, the little river which ran between the southern tip of Lake Lodoga and its eastward sister Lake Onega but would not come further to meet them (the Svir, in any case, is only just beyond the 1939 Russia-Finnish frontier) and would make no more than a demonstration towards Leningrad from Karelia. Thoroughly put out, Keitel of OKW flew to see Mannerheim on 4th September hoping to persuade him otherwise. But Mannerheim continued to argue that he 'lacked the strength' to press any further towards Leningrad. While it was true that the line of the frontier was guarded by permanent defences, it was clear to all that his real reason for declining to attack it was political: however unlikely it might seem at that moment that Finland would ever have to deal again with a resurgent Russia, caution demanded that she behave no more predatorily to-

wards Russia than Russia had done towards her after at the end of the war, the year before. On such unspoken conventions do the most important international understandings rest.

Army Group North had thus to find the means to complete the encirclement of Leningrad from its own resources. On 5th September these were proportionately diminished by the announcement, in Führer Directive 35, that the capture of Moscow must forthwith be regarded as the most pressing priority; a change of plan – or reversion to an original plan – which entailed the transfer of most of Leeb's armour to Army Group Centre in order to accelerate its drive along the high road to Moscow. The immediate approaches to Leningrad, from the South, moreover, were prodigiously well-protected, being covered by three separate lines of obstacles and prepared positions. The Germans had breached the first of these lines on 19th August to 21st, but the second and third remained. Already formidable, they were under constant improvement by the people of Leningrad.

Despite the strength of these defences – it has been claimed that

127

Below: Russians manning the outposts of the Leningrad defence line. *Above:* A column of obsolete Russian tanks moving into position outside Leningrad. *Left:* A Russian column passing the Admiralty building

Above: Heavy anti-aircraft gun in
central Leningrad. Left: Russians under
fire in the marshes of the Neva

they comprised 620 miles of earth
walls, 400 miles of anti-tank ditches,
285 miles of wooden abatis, 5,000
pillboxes and 370 miles of barbed wire
entanglements – Leeb decided to
attempt a direct assault. He was
probably aware that this was contrary
to Hitler's wishes, for though Hitler
had not promulgated a final decision
about the future of Leningrad – he had
talked both of compelling its three
million inhabitants to flee across open
country into Russian lines and of
allowing them to starve to death
within the city – his wish to avoid a
street battle was generally known at
Leeb's level in the Army. Beginning on
8th September, therefore, Army Group
North, now minus most of its tanks
(XXXIX Corps remained with it but
Panzergruppe 4 had begun the move to
join Bock) started to drive into the
Russian lines. On this first day, it
secured its most important success,

the capture of Schlusselburg on Lake
Ladoga, which cut Leningrad off from
communication overland with the rest
of Russia. It could henceforth only be
approached by water across Lake
Ladoga.

Thereafter the fighting progressed
very much more slowly. On 11th September the Germans secured a foot-
hold on the Dudernof heights, which
gave them a commanding view across
'the golden cupolas and towers' from
that point, only seven-and-a-half
miles distant from the centre of the
city. The fighting was so severe, however, (one panzer division had its
commander wounded and replaced
three times on 10th September) that
Hitler felt compelled to allow the
panzer divisions earmarked for Bock
to remain a little longer with Leeb.
But on 17th September he insisted that
they must go eastward, and from that
moment the German attack lost its
impetus. For this turn of events,
however, the Russians could thank
themselves quite as much as Hitler.
They had fought with extraordinary

131

Above: Building barricades in the heart of Leningrad. *Left:* Waiting to be evacuated across the 'Ice Road'

tenacity, with some skill and with what appeared to be a total unconcern for losses either of men or equipment. How had their defence been so successfully organised?

In part, it had been due to the unusually high level of political organisation already existing in the city: about 200,000 of its inhabitants belonged to the Communist Party and 300,000 to the Young Communist League, making in all about one person in six an initiate of party methods of administration control. Many others would also have belonged to the *Osoaviakhim* and some, of course, would have belonged to both. There was, therefore, a large nucleus of citizens trained and ready to carry out emergency duties. Besides these, there was a high proportion of industrial workers in the city, already closely organised, and, beyond that, the Party leadership in the city could count upon a strong fund of local

patriotism among the ordinary citizens.

One of the first measures to harness this considerable force of trained and untrained manpower in the defence of the city was taken on 27th June, when the Leningrad City Soviet (the equivalent of a city council in America or Britain) issued a decree mobilising the entire population of men between sixteen and fifty and women between sixteen and forty-five for defence work. The numbers theoretically made available by such a decree were naturally too large to be employed in any useful way and the city Soviet did not, in practice, call the population forward *en masse*. Nevertheless, it did conscript considerable bodies of the younger and fitter as soon as the threat to Leningrad became manifest in early July and turned their labour to the construction of the triple ring of fortifications around the city. In advance of these, a double line of lesser fortifications had already been dug, and was added to during the crisis period, while from August onwards an elaborate system of barricades, road-

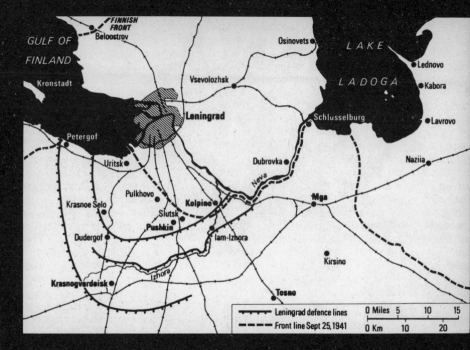

GULF OF FINLAND
FINNISH FRONT
Beloostrov
Osinovets
LAKE LADOGA
Kronstadt
Vsevolozhsk
Lednovo
Kabora
Leningrad
Lavrovo
Petergof
Schlusselburg
Uritsk
Dubrovka
Naziia
Neva
Pulkhovo
Krasnoe Selo
Kolpine
Mga
Slutsk
Pushkin
Dudergof
Iam-Izhora
Izhora
Kirsino
Krasnogvardeisk
Tosno

Leningrad defence lines
Front line Sept 25, 1941

0 Miles   5   10   15
0 Km   10   20

Leningrad defences

locks and concealed pillboxes and trongpoints was built in the outlying istricts of the city. 'Inevitably those onscripted suffered considerable tardships at the work of fortification. The people who had to do the work vere frequently unaccustomed to such abour. They often had to work for welve to fifteen hours at a stretch, leep in barns or lean-tos, and occasionally were subjected to enemy are. Sometimes they were even overun by a sudden enemy advance. In other cases they completed one assignment only to start an immediate orced march of six to twelve miles to another construction site. Most of the ime they had only the simplest hand ools. Frequently women had to manandle the heavy concrete obstacles that were constructed against tanks. Many of the people lacked proper working clothes and shoes. Girls and women often came in light summer dresses and shoes.' Despite these discomforts and fatigues, the labour gangs worked with tremendous heart; and to considerable purpose, for the fortifications, though they were not to prove wholly impenetrable, did confine the final German breakthrough to Leningrad to a front too narrow to permit them to develop a successful assault on the city.

Leningrad had to provide from its own resources for its active as well as passive defence and, because of the heavy losses suffered by the regular divisions outside the city during July and August, the formations raised from its population were to play a decisive role in decelerating and eventually halting the German advance. There were a number of these formations. The first group, known as Destruction Battalions and intended to take on enemy parachutists, were organised from 24th June onwards, and had reached a strength of 17,000 men by 5th July. By that date, however, the city was on the way to creating a far more considerable force, a Militia Army of 200,000 organised into fifteen divisions. It was a plan which proved over-ambitious, since to have enlisted so many would have been to reduce the output of Leningrad's many and very important factories below an effective level, but it did produce very quickly, which is to say between 5th and 15th July, three divisions – the 1st, 2nd and 3rd *Opolchenie* – which, though untrained and under-equipped and led for the most part by party nominees who were only sometimes also reserve officers, were committed almost immediately to battle. A fourth division was raised on 19th July.

Shortly afterwards Voroshilov, commanding on the Northern Front, decided that future *Opolchenie* divisions would carry the title 'Guards' a word which had been out of favour since the revolution. Four of these were formed between 24th July and 13th August and all swiftly despatched to the front, which was now rapidly closing on the city. Stalin was later to adopt this idea of Voroshilov's to better use, by conferring the 'Guards' title on units which had performed outstandingly in action. It was to become a greatly coveted honour.

Yet despite all Leningrad did to help itself, it could not stave off the German onset, nor prevent its own isolation from the rest of Russia. In mid-September, moreover, it looked as if the defenders of the city were about to be overwhelmed in the final German assault. Krasnoe Selo, the Russian Versailles, fell to the Germans on 10th September, and on 14th September the leading tanks of XLI Panzer Corps broke through the last of the triple ring of fortifications at the Pulkovo heights and stood poised to descend into the heart of the city.

In practice, it was not to be allowed to do so. Hitler, after long indecision, had at last arrived at the view that Leningrad should not be assaulted. Its size, the strength of its buildings (being a Western style city, and one built on a monumental scale, its public and many of its private buildings were far more solidly constructed than those in most other Russian

Victims of German shelling on the Nevski Prospect

cities), and its many canals made it a military obstacle of the first order, one which threatened to engulf very large numbers of troops for little material result. Leeb, commanding Army Group North, nevertheless attempted a *coup de main* between 6th and 14th September, the initial success of which compelled Hitler temporarily to suspend the effect of Directive No 35, which had ordered the transfer of all armour to Army Group Centre, but its failure, which had become evident by 14th September, caused him to re-impose his ban on a penetration of the city in force. It was enough, he judged, that Leningrad be tightly invested. Its buildings were then to be destroyed by air and artillery bombardment and such of its inhabitants who escaped death by these means were to be allowed to starve.

During the winter of 1941-2 nearly a million Leningraders were to die of starvation, cold or of the diseases brought on by those conditions. Despite the construction of an 'ice-road' across Lake Ladoga, it proved impossible to ferry into the city supplies enough to provide even those fighting at the front with what is normally regarded as the minimum necessary to sustain life. Those in less important work received consonantly less and those unable to work, particularly the old who had to remain in their freezing houses, were allotted purely token amounts. Despite these appalling experiences, the population of Leningrad were never to flinch from their resolve, which they had shown from the beginning, to defend their city whatever the cost. That resolve, which forced the Germans first to commit and then to sustain important forces on the northern front for some time longer than sober military judgement would have allowed, was a major factor in frustrating Hitler's final endeavour for 1941: the capture of Moscow.

137

Defeat before the gates of Moscow

Before Kiev had fallen (15th September) and Leningrad been completely encircled (8th September), Hitler had at last yielded to those arguments – but also to his own inner promptings – which urged that the German Army, or the *Ostheer* which formed its major part, should abandon what was coming increasingly to look like the peripheral campaigns on the northern and southern wings ·and concentrate its reserves, its supplies, above all its armour, for a final drive against Moscow. The arguments and promptings spoke thus: Moscow remained the focus of Russian military communications, the centre of Russian civil government, the symbol of

Russian resistance. To attack Moscow must compel the Russians, on strategic, on political and on emotional grounds, to concentrate the best of what forces they had left – and despite their capacity to conjure new divisions into being, German intelligence reckoned those forces to be few – in defence of the capital. The battle which would ensue would, the Germans judged and hoped, destroy the Red Army as a fighting force and end the eastern war at a single blow.

Führer Directive 35, which conveyed the news of Hitler's change of mind to his Army Group Commanders, did not state so sweeping a set of claims for the operation. It merely laid down

armour, he was to have three marching armies, the Ninth, Fourth and Second.

Their immediate aim was to encircle as much as possible of the 'Timoshenko Army Group'. The operation was to take the form of a double envelopment, the pincers to meet east of Viasma, which would bring the leading tanks to within little more than a hundred miles of Moscow, on the main road to the capital from the west. Guderian's Panzergruppe 2 – or more properly his Second Panzer Army, as it had been re-named – was to attempt a similar envelopment 'south-east of Roslavl' (meaning around Briansk), by sweeping with its tanks north-eastward to effect a junction with the infantry of Second Army, which was to advance due east. These objectives or dispositions were given final form in the Army Group operation order (code-named 'Typhoon') which Bock issued on 19th September. It was now only a matter of assembling the necessary force of men and material, but the task of reinforcement and even more so of supply had now begun to be beset by grim difficulties. The railways, though operating on the main lines as far forward as Smolensk and Roslavl, which were places still close behind the front line, were working far below peacetime capacity. Only ten thousand miles, little enough in a countryside the area of western Russia, had been converted to the western gauge. Railways were vital to the preparation of an offensive, since Russia did not possess the road network nor the German army the trucks which would have allowed it to amass supplies by road in quantities and at the necessary speed to fulfil Hitler's timetable for the battle. Many of the existing trucks, moreover, were by this stage of the campaign verging on breakdown, as were many of the armoured vehicles,

that an attack was to be organised against the Timoshenko Army Group (i.e. the Russian Western Front), to begin at the earliest possible moment, estimated to be late September. In order to provide it with the necessary might and penetrative power, both Army Groups North and South were to transfer important forces to Bock's control. These 'important forces' were Hoepner's Panzergruppe 4, detached from Army Group North, and Guderian's Panzergruppe 2, returned from Army Group South. Bock would therefore dispose of three Panzergruppen, these two and Hoth's Gruppe 3, which had also been assisting Leeb's advance in Leningrad: besides the

the enormous distances they had had to cover in marching and counter-marching on detached missions having taken a severe toll. Spare parts were needed in quantity, since many panzer divisions were down to less than a quarter of their tank establishment.

In the event, sufficient reinforcements and supplies were brought forward to allow Bock to begin his offensive more or less on time, on 2nd October. The Russians opposite Bock's concentration, who were almost without benefit of air reconnaissance, were taken by surprise, and since their numbers were considerably fewer than their order of battle would have suggested, began at once to yield ground. The Russians belonged to one of three Army Groups: Western, command of which had been taken by Koniev from Timoshenko since Hitler's Directive No 35 had been issued; Briansk, commanded by Yeremenko; and the Reserve Front, now commanded by Zhukov, who doled out reinforcements from it with a niggardly hand. In all, the Russians held Bock's front of attack with fifteen Armies; their combined strength, however, did not reach half a million men, many of whom were reservists or conscripts, fresh from the village street. Despite their arrangement in depth – Zhukov kept four Armies on the Viasma Line, so-called, throughout the fighting – the Russian defence was therefore not particularly effective; indeed, in a number of respects which were to emerge after the fighting had begun, it was organised so as to assist rather than resist a successful German attack.

The German attack opened promptly on 2nd October and quickly penetrated the Russian front. By 7th October, by subsequent Russian testimony, the main forces of their Western and Reserve Fronts – Nineteenth, Twenty-Fourth, Thirtieth and Thirty-Second Armies – had been surrounded,

Koniev, one of the victors of the Battle of Moscow

trapped between Viasma and Smolensk by the fast-moving panzer wings of Bock's main concentration. Of the 7th October situation, Zhukov was later to write 'All roads to Moscow were in essence open', an admission of the extent of Russian helplessness in the face of the determined and well-planned German attack. Their trapped soldiers, though they had fought and continued to fight from within the pocket with great courage, had lacked the skill to mount the sort of sharp, co-ordinated counter-attack which alone can throw an experienced enemy off his balance and tumble him backwards. They were also, of course, very short of heavy weapons and armoured vehicles.

Guderian simultaneously had brought off a similar encirclement in the southern half of Army Group Centre's front, around the city of Briansk. A column of his Panzer-gruppe 2, directed northwards for his advance on Orel, made contact with the marching infantry of Second Army on 9th October, thus surrounding and eventually subduing completely two other Russian Armies, the Third and Thirteenth. In all, the Germans claimed as a result of these two battles, Viasma-Briansk, the capture of 657,000 prisoners, 1,241 tanks and 5,396 pieces of artillery. The Russians, moreover, had on many occasions shown little fighting spirit and had given themselves up easily: on this piece of intelligence Hitler was to base a very over-optimistic forecast of the prospects of his advance on Moscow.

Had he been 'reading' the battle with an open mind, he would have found evidence of the quality of the Russians' combativeness of a quite contrary sort. Guderian, visiting his 4th Panzer Division on 8th October, following an engagement on 6th October when T-34s had appeared for the first time against his troops, found that 'descriptions . . . of the new tactical handling of the Russian tanks were very worrying. Our defensive weapons available at that period were

only successful against the T-34 when the conditions were unusually favourable. The short-barrelled 75mm gun of the Panzer IV was only effective if the T-34 was attacked from the rear; even then a hit had to be scored on the grating above the engine to knock it out. It required very great skill to manoeuvre into a position from which such a shot was possible. The Russians attacked us frontally with infantry, while they sent their tanks in, in mass formations, against our flanks. They were learning'. Even more ominously he noted in his war diary on 6th October the first snowfall of the approaching winter. It melted quickly, leaving the roads once again liquid with mud. Difficult to know, at this stage of the campaign and time of the year, which was preferable: a prolonged autumn, with the attendant rainfall which so hampered movement, or an early frost which might harden the ground quickly enough to permit a dash at the final objective – or herald the blizzards. Either way, it was out of Hitler's hands.

On the Russian side, such encouraging signs were swamped by the effect of this renewed current of disaster. It led to the creation – by decree rather than physical preparation – of a new and 'final' defensive line, the Mozhaisk Line, forty miles to the west of Moscow, and to the appointment of yet another commander to the Western Front – but this time of a commander with a genuine if as yet only partially revealed mastery of war: Zhukov.

Zhukov, the cavalryman of the Civil War and the armoured attack specialist of the Russo-Japanese Manchurian border campaign, was now called upon to direct what could only be a strategy

Above: The reconnaissance element of an infantry position has just made contact with Russian rearguards during the breakthrough at Viasma
Below: A troop of Panzer Mk III Js with the new long 50mm gun in the advance from Viasma

143

of retreat, or of 'yielding defence' as theoreticians would call it. Ticklish enough to organise with fresh and well-equipped troops – Guderian pronounced it an invariable recipe for confusion – it was to be a strategy of the very greatest difficulty to implement with the broken remnants which were all that Smolensk and Viasma-Briansk had left him. He could draw a little comfort, however, from the pattern which the German attack seemed to be following. It was least assertive in the centre, on the main Moscow-Minsk road, where the continued resistance of the six armies encircled in the Viasma pocket was preventing any quick advance down that road by Panzergruppe 4, or Ninth Army. On the flanks, the axis which led towards Kalinin in the north, on which Panzergruppe 3 was moving, and Tula in the south, Guderian's objective, there were still organised, if not numerous, Russian covering forces. It was his hope therefore, that these twin pincers, which threatened to encircle Moscow, could be delayed long enough for the arrival of winter – the blizzards were due in six weeks – and of reinforcements to stop them in their tracks.

This hope was to be dissipated instantaneously by the events of 14th October; when Hoth's Panzergruppe 3 broke through the Russian screen on

the northern axis and swept into Kalinin, and through it to the Sea of Moscow, the artificial lake seventy miles north of the city. The news, shattering enough to the High Command, could not be kept from the citizens of the capital and provoked, on 16th October and the days following, a panic and an exodus which was only halted by ruthless security measures. Vast numbers – perhaps half a million – of Muscovites were at forced labour on the western defences at this moment and could not, even had they wished, have beaten any sort of retreat. It was among unsupervised stay-at-homes that morale cracked.

Although the situation was to worsen, civilian morale strongly improved after this sudden crisis. The improvement was due to many factors, among which must be counted Stalin's very remarkable speech to the troops in Red Square on the anniversary of the October Revolution, which invoked, in a style of which no Marxist theoretician could have approved, all the national heroes of Russian – pre-, post-, and even anti-Revolutionary – in a calculated, and by and large very successful, attempt to persuade his listeners that the war was a patriotic one to be fought for

Russians captured outside Moscow, November 1941

Above: The first snow. The transport of the infantry divisions was still wholly horse-drawn. *Below:* Germans advance through Kalinin, captured 14th October

Russia by all Russians, not merely for Communism by Party members.

But speeches do not halt tanks. And thin on the ground though the Panzers were becoming, the Germans spearheads continued to thrust towards Moscow along the northern and southern flanks – towards Klin and Istra, towards Tula and Stalinogorsk. Movement was desperately slow by Panzer standards, however, for not only did the Russians, though desperately weakened, contest their advance every foot of the way, but the roads remained liquid and the countryside waterlogged. Not until the beginning of November did the first sharp frosts of the winter harden the ground sufficiently for the High Command to think seriously about organising its final dash towards the towers and cupolas of the Kremlin, now only forty miles distant.

They had to reckon with a very grave diminution in the fighting power of their forces. Although the marching divisions still retained some sixty-five per cent of their complements, the infantry strength of the Panzer and motorised divisions had declined by half – and these 'tank-followers' were vital to the progress of the tanks – while their tank strength had declined by sixty-five per cent. It was with these figures in mind that the German Army high command met at Orsha, Army Group Centre's headquarters, on 13th November. Present were Halder, Chief of the General Staff, and various Chiefs of Staff of corps and armies. Such a conference between deputies rather than commanders was very much part of the German military system, in which Chiefs of Staff enjoyed a remarkable measure of power and independence. The question put to them by Halder was a simple one: should the Germans proceed with their

Right: Building tank traps in the Stalin Line. *Below right:* A steel barricade goes up in Moscow, November 1941. The fire is to thaw the soil

offensive, or should they accept that the imminent arrival of 'General December' make it wiser to dig in for the winter? Sodenstern, Chief of Staff to Runstedt at Army Group South, was the first to reply: he argued for an immediate halt, at least in the Ukraine where the German spearheads had penetrated so much more deeply than anywhere else and now risked being cut off if not allowed to consolidate their gains. Griffenberg, Leeb's Chief of Staff at Army Group North, spoke for a command which had already become static: he argued for a halt also. Only Bock's Chief of Staff, Brennecke, would advance arguments for continuing the offensive on Moscow, which he described as a military and psychological necessity. 'The danger that we might not succeed' he added 'must be taken into account, but it would be even worse to be left lying in the snow and the cold on open ground thirty miles from the tempting objective'. Halder concurred. As it happened, Hitler had already decided that the final stage of the offensive would take place so that the Orsha Conference partook of the character of a counting of heads rather than of an executive session. The division of opinion it revealed, however, was of the very greatest interest to the high command, as it is to students of the campaign.

The final stage of the advance on Moscow began on 16th November. For this stage of the campaign, Bock had shifted Panzergruppe 4 rather backward on its axis towards Panzergruppe 3 (now commanded by Reinhardt). This left Kluge's Fourth Army, weak in armour, a rather broader front than before, and Guderian's Panzergruppe 2 very much on its own. The general direction of the German advance was north-east and its object, as obvious to the Russians as to the best-informed

German staff officer, to encircle Moscow by a double envelopment.

Despite the arrival of some reinforcements of men and material from the interior, and the elimination of most of the incompetent commanders, the Russians were at first unable to stop this German thrust on any broad front. At Tula, which Guderian was making a second go of capturing, the garrison was able to drive his army for the outskirts, threatening him with losses he did not choose to accept, but he merely swung his armoured columns around the town and adopted a more directly northerly stab at the approaches to Moscow. And on the northern flank, where the Russians were struggling to consolidate a defensive line along the Volga Canal and the Sea of Moscow, Ninth Army was nevertheless able to break through to the canal line while Panzergruppe 3 made touch with it south of Dimitrov roughly at the same time on 27th November. On 28th November the 7th Panzer Division was actually able to establish a bridgehead on the far bank but desperate Russian counterattacks nullified any prospect of developing a break-out from it.

The German effort was now at crisis point. At Krasnaya Polyana, on Panzergruppe 3's front, they stood only eighteen miles from Moscow; Fourth Army, with its outposts at Burtsevo, was only twenty-five miles from the city; Guderian was sixty-nine miles away, to the south. Legend has it that German troops were to approach close enough in the days following to see the towers of the Kremlin gleaming in a burst of evening sunshine, and that some patrols even got into the outlying suburbs of Moscow. If they did, their forays were the last flickers of energy in an army expiring on its feet. The Russian winter in all its cruelty, unknown and unimaginable to a westerner, was now attacking in earnest, and the losses

The onset of winter restored freedom of movement to the German armour

it inflicted, allied to those which a still strenuously resistant and now strongly reinforced Red Army could cause, brought one German attack after another to a halt. Guderian's Panzergruppe made no further progress after its run at Kashira on 25th November, in a last effort to break through to the east of Moscow and take the city from the rear. Two days later Guderian ordered a withdrawal. And after 29th November there was virtually no further forward movement either by Ninth Army or Panzergruppe 3. Bock, writing to Halder on 1st December, explained his Army Group's predicament. 'After further bloody struggles the offensive will bring a restricted gain of ground and it will destroy part of the enemy's forces, but it is most unlikely to bring about strategical success. The idea that the enemy facing the Army Group was on the point of collapse was, as the fighting of the last fortnight shows, a pipe-dream. To remain outside the gates of Moscow, where the rail and road systems connect with almost the whole of eastern Russia, means heavy defensive fighting for us against an enemy vastly superior in numbers. Further offensive action therefore seems to be senseless and aimless, especially as the time is coming very near when the physical strength of the troops will be completely exhausted.'

That moment in fact had already arrived. The ordinary German soldiers of the fighting divisions were now almost incapable of movement, let alone combat. They were for the vast majority quite without winter clothing of any sort, having only their overcoats, which offered little protection against the piercing winds off the steppe, and being forced to wear their tightfitting and steel-shod jackboots, which almost guaranteed frostbite in the feet. Frostbite cases were now more numerous than wounds in the field hospitals and, because Hitler had refused to allow the provision of winter clothing lest evidence of pre-

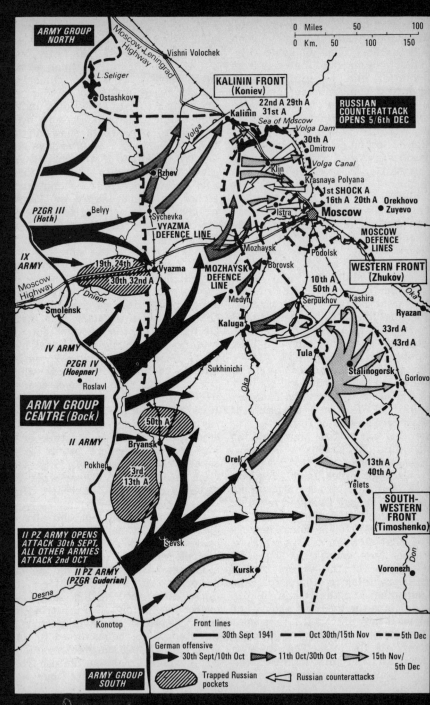

The final German advance on Moscow and the opening of the Russian counter-offensive, 30th September – 5th December, 1941

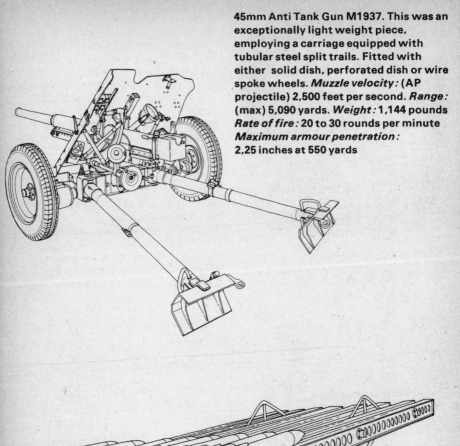

45mm Anti Tank Gun M1937. This was an exceptionally light weight piece, employing a carriage equipped with tubular steel split trails. Fitted with either solid dish, perforated dish or wire spoke wheels. *Muzzle velocity:* (AP projectile) 2,500 feet per second. *Range:* (max) 5,090 yards. *Weight:* 1,144 pounds *Rate of fire:* 20 to 30 rounds per minute *Maximum armour penetration:* 2,25 inches at 550 yards

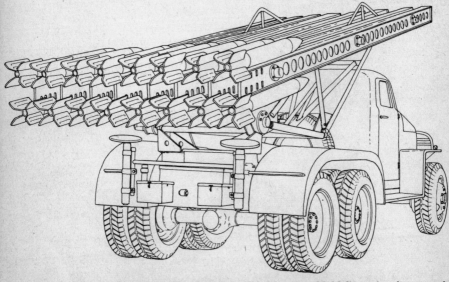

132mm Rocket Launcher M.13. The Soviet rocket launcher M.13 fires simultaneously 16 rounds of 132mm finstabilized rockets from a multi-rail rocket launcher mounted on a 6 by 6 truck. The rockets were positioned. 8 resting on the guide rails and 8 slung below, and were fired electrically from the drivers cab. *Range:* 9,700 yards

paration for a winter campaign depress morale, it' was certain that the incidence of frostbite would continue to rise. The troops, of course, had begun to improvise, notably by wearing their denim fatigue uniforms over their service dress and stuffing the space between with screwed-up paper, but improvisation could not save the *Ostheer* from the Russian winter.

The Russian winter, on the other hand, would do much to help the Red Army. The winter months were traditionally its most destructive weapon against an invader, but the snow and cloud also provided a valuable screen behind which reinforcements might be

Below: A Ski battalion leaving for the front, Moscow, December 1941
Left: Sorge, Master Spy and Hero of the Soviet Union

assembled. Hitherto it had been of little use, for reinforcements were not to be had. But suddenly reinforcements had become available in quantities and Zhukov was marshalling these for a counter-stroke, which would save Moscow. The story of how he had come to be given these divisions is a fascinating one.

Russia had, even in Czarist times, maintained a large army in Siberia, to guard her frontiers with China, Manchuria, Mongolia and Korea. It was this army, later reinforced along the Trans-Siberian railway, which had fought the Japanese in 1904-5. The Soviet government had retained and ultimately added to this Far Eastern Army which, under Marshal Blucher, was eventually to achieve a semi-autonomous status – as well as a very high level of efficiency. It was

twice to fight the Japanese, with whom the Soviet government was in constant disagreement about the exact demarcation of the frontier between Russian protected Mongolia and Japanese occupied China, on the last occasion on a major scale at the battle of Khalkhin Gol.

Thereafter, though remaining on diplomatic speaking terms with the Japanese, the Russians regarded them as potential aggressors 'and maintained the Far Eastern Army at the very highest state of readiness and equipment. Its strength always stood between thirty and forty divisions, with a powerful complement of tanks and aircraft. And throughout the disasters of the summer and early autumn of 1941, at that strength the Far Eastern Army remained.

From July onwards, however, the Kremlin had been receiving reports that Japan might be on the verge of an offensive so vast in scale and so remote from Russian territory in its objectives that a transfer of strength from Siberia to the west might after all be contemplated. These reports emanated from a very remarkable man, Richard Sorge, now a posthumous Hero of the Soviet Union, then an apparently patriotic and keenly Nazi German journalist working in Tokyo.

Sorge was certainly German, but his politics were communist and he had been for many years a professional agent of Russian Intelligence. He had been able to set up an excellent cover and to penetrate both the German Embassy, which he did himself by getting on intimate terms with the Ambassador, and the Japanese cabinet, through a collaborator. In this way he was able to get word of the impending Japanese attack on Pearl Harbor and pass it to Moscow, perhaps as early as 3rd October. Even more remarkably – for credibility is perhaps the most difficult quality for an agent to establish – he got his reports believed. Thus it was that from October onwards, at first in trickles and then eventually in a flood, reinforcements were bought from Siberia to defend Moscow. They were excellent troops, well-trained and equipped and above all clothed for and immune to the coldest of winters.

Out of these reinforcements, which may have amounted to as much as eighteen divisions, with 1700 tanks and 1500 aircraft – Zhukov was able to form three new armies, the First Shock, the Tenth and the Twentieth. Koniev, commanding the new Kalinin Front formed from the Twenty-Second, Twenty-Ninth and Thirty-First Armies, was holding successfully around the Sea of Moscow and the Volga Canal. Zhukov now intended

to launch his fresh troops westward, from starting points north and south of Moscow, and repay the Germans in their own coin for the losses the Russians had suffered in the battles of encirclement during the summer.

The plan, agreed between the field and central staffs and ultimately approved by Stalin, called for an attack by three Fronts: Kalinin, (Koniev), Western (Zhukov) and South - Western (Timoshenko). Zhukov's Front was to make the main effort. On its northern wing its First Shock and Twentieth Armies, both fresh, were to lead an attack, also to be mounted by the Thirtieth and Sixteenth Armies, straight into the

Panzergruppen's positions and attempt to make a junction with the Thirty-First and Twenty-Ninth Armies of Koniev's Kalinin Front. The central section of Zhukov's Front was to act so offensively as to retain in place the German troops opposite it, whilst the southern wing, the Fiftieth and Tenth Armies, in co-operation with Timoshenko's South-western Front, were to strike at Guderian's Panzergruppe.

The attack was launched on 6th December, two days after Kluge, commanding the Fourth Army, had decided to give up any further offensive effort and one day after Guderian had come to the same decision. The initial pace of the advance was not rapid, but it gathered momentum steadily. In the north, the deepest advance on the first day was made by Lelyushenko's Thirtieth Army, which advanced as far as the Moscow-Leningrad highway, threatening Panzergruppe 3's liaison with Fourth Army. By 9th December, it had reached Klin and with his First Schock Army seemed poised to bring off an encirclement. Sixteenth and Twentieth Armies, under Rokossovsky and Vlasov respectively (the first

Russian assault pioneers cut gaps in German entanglements under fire Moscow, December 1941

destined to become a Marshal and Hero of the Soviet Union, the second to lead an emigré army against his homeland and die reviled as a traitor) matched their progress. By 13th December, these columns had retaken Istra.

At the same time the Russian formations opposite Guderian were making even more promising inroads into the German positions. Thirteenth and Fortieth Armies, belonging to Timoshenko's south-western front, had broken into the southern face of the salient which Panzergruppe 3 had opened up in November, and by 9th December were menacing its main line of supply, the Orel-Tula railway. Meanwhile the Fiftieth and Tenth Armies were attacking on the northern face of the salient and were succeeding in widening a gap they had created between Guderian's left flank and Kluge's right. Unrelenting pressure resulted in a steady displacement of Kluge's Fourth Army westward, accelerated after 18th December when the Thirty-Third and Forty-Third Armies joined in the offensive.

The news from the other Russian Fronts was equally encouraging. In the far south, Runstedt's (dangerously over-extended) Army Group had been driven out of Rostov-on-Don, which it captured on 23rd November, on 28th November and subsequently chased as far west as the River Mius where it managed to re-establish a line and dig in for the winter. In the north, Koniev's Kalinin Front, after a desperately hard struggle against the German Ninth Army, recaptured the city from which it took its name, and pressed on south-westward along the line of the upper Volga towards Rzhev.

By Christmas Day, 1941, the Russian armies had regained almost all the territory taken by the Germans in the final stage of their Moscow offensive. It might, therefore, be judged a failure, and Moscow, in consequence, saved. Hitler himself certainly took that view. On 8th December he had issued Führer Directive No 39 which decreed a defensive posture on the eastern front, as a result of the advent of winter and of 'the consequent difficulty in bringing up supplies'. On 17th December his propaganda machine announced that the front might have to be shortened in places, an admission that retreat was taking place and would continue to do so. But Hitler was by no means prepared to sanction retreat as a means of absorbing the impetus of the Russian advance. Indeed, though many of his generals were to beg for permission to withdraw to positions where they might better shelter and supply their troops, he set his face against it, insisting that any assent by the High Command to a general retreat would result inevitably in a repetition of the disasters of 1812, when Napoleon's army had been destroyed by the blizzards and the Cossacks.

Since he could not trust his commanders to take him at his word when he forbade retreat, he emphasised the force of his determination by a round of dismissals. The most important of these – that of Brauchitsch, the Commander-in-Chief whose post he assumed himself – completed that subjection of the army to his personal control upon which he had embarked in 1934. The other dismissals were in the nature of a punishment of those who had failed him in the field: Leeb and Bock were both relieved; so too was Guderian, the most insubordinate if indispensable Panzer commander; Hoepner also, whom Hitler had cashiered; while Runstedt was transferred to a quiet command in the west. Thirty-five corps or divisional commanders were removed at the same time. There had not been so drastic a purge of commanders (outside Russia, of course) since Joffre had sacked half his generals in 1914.

The parallel between the French campaign of 1914 and the Russian campaign of 1941 may profitably be taken further, since the reasons for the initial disasters which overtook

the defenders in each case are, in some respects, closely similar (if very dissimilar in others). Both the French and Russian armies were schooled in a very defective tactical doctrine. Both lacked the support which frontier fortifications would have lent their defence (the Russians because they were occupying foreign territory of their fortified frontier, the French because they proclaimed a contempt for static positions however strong). Both deployed their armies in a fashion which, since it lacked depth in reserves, made the task of the enemy infinitely easier than it should have been.

The reasons for the two armies' recovery also betray similarities. Both overstretched their enemy by retaining their cohesion throughout a long retreat. Both sustained the morale of their soldiers in an astonishing fashion. Both used their capital cities as a bastion from which to launch a decisive counter-attack at the crucial moment. But having pointed to these similarities, one must not be tempted to push them too far. Agonising though the ordeal of the French army was during the Battle of the Frontiers and the Retreat to

A column of Panzer Mk IIs leaving Rostov, December 1941, after its brief occupation by the Germans

the Marne in 1914, the extent of its sufferings and the unexpectedness of its recovery cannot be measured on the same scale as that on which we must measure the Russian army's. Nearly four million prisoners had fallen into German hands and two million Russian soldiers died or received wounds before the Battle of Moscow began. That the remnants of the Red Army preserved their strength and the faith to turn-about, to check and finally repel the German invaders is a measure of the enormous resilience of the Russian, of his deep love of country and of the hatred which the Germans had already inspired in his breast.

Yet the Battle of Moscow was to prove not even the beginning of the road to victory. The Russians would have to suffer another year of disaster and retreat before they could set their feet westward, to repossess the scorched earth of their homeland and bring deliverance to the survivors of the German occupation.

159

Bibliography

The Soviet Army by Sir Basil Liddell Hart (Weidenfeld and Nicolson, London)

Russia at War by Alexander Werth (Barrie and Rockliff, London. Dutton, New York)

Panzer Leader by General Heinz Guderian (Michael Joseph, London. Ballantine Books, New York)

Juggernaut by Malcolm Mackintosh (Secker and Warburg, London. Macmillan, New York)

Barbarossa by Alan Clark (Hutchinson, London. New American Library, New York)

The Nemesis of Power by Sir John Wheeler-Bennett (Macmillan, London. Viking Press, New York)

Marshal Zhukov's Greatest Battles by Georgi K Zhukov (Macdonald, London. Harper and Row, New York)

Hitler's War Directives by H R Trevor-Roper (Sidgwick and Jackson, London)